Potential Situational Interview Questions and Answers for the Role of HR Manager

1. Q: How would you handle a situation where an employee is consistently late for work?

A: I would first have a private conversation with the employee to understand the reasons behind their tardiness. If there are valid reasons, such as personal issues or transportation problems, I would work with them to find a solution. If the tardiness persists without a justifiable cause, I would follow the company's disciplinary procedures, which may include verbal warnings, written warnings, and eventually, termination if the behavior does not improve.

2. Q: An employee comes to you with a complaint about their manager. How would you address this situation?

A: I would listen to the employee's concerns and gather all relevant information. I would then discuss the issue with the manager to get their perspective. If necessary, I would facilitate a meeting between the employee and the manager to resolve the issue. If the complaint is serious, such as harassment or discrimination, I would involve upper management and follow the company's policies and procedures for handling such situations.

3. Q: How would you handle a situation where two employees are in conflict with each other?

A: I would meet with both employees separately to understand their perspectives and the root cause of the conflict. I would then bring them together for a mediation session, where I would facilitate a discussion to help them find common ground and develop a solution. If the conflict persists, I would work with their manager to develop a plan of action, which may include training, counseling, or disciplinary measures.

4. Q: An employee is not meeting performance expectations. How would you address this situation?

A: I would first review the employee's job description and performance goals to ensure that expectations are clear. I would then meet with the employee and their manager to discuss the performance issues and develop a performance improvement plan (PIP). The PIP would outline specific goals, timelines, and support resources. I would monitor the employee's progress and provide regular feedback and coaching. If the employee does not improve after the PIP, I would follow the company's disciplinary procedures, which may include termination.

5. Q: How would you handle a situation where an employee is found to be under the influence of drugs or alcohol at work?

A: I would immediately remove the employee from the workplace to ensure the safety of themselves and others. I would then follow the company's drug and alcohol policy, which may include drug testing, referral to an employee assistance program (EAP), and disciplinary action, up to and including termination. I would also document the incident and involve upper management as necessary.

6. Q: An employee requests a leave of absence due to a personal issue. How would you handle this request?

A: I would first review the company's leave policies to determine the employee's eligibility for leave. I would then meet with the employee to understand their situation and the duration of leave needed. If the employee is eligible for leave, I would assist them in completing the necessary paperwork and ensure that their job duties are covered during their absence. I would also maintain communication with the employee during their leave and assist with their transition back to work.

7. Q: How would you handle a situation where an employee is not following safety protocols?

A: I would immediately address the situation with the employee and remind them of the importance of following safety protocols. I would provide additional training if necessary and document the incident. If the employee continues to violate safety protocols, I would follow the company's disciplinary procedures, which may include verbal warnings, written warnings, and eventually, termination if the behavior does not improve.

8. Q: An employee complains that they are being harassed by a coworker. How would you address this situation?

A: I would take the complaint seriously and immediately investigate the situation. I would interview the employee, the accused coworker, and any witnesses. If the investigation confirms harassment, I would take appropriate disciplinary action against the accused coworker, up to and including termination. I would also provide support resources to the employee who made the complaint and ensure that they are protected from retaliation.

9. Q: How would you handle a situation where an employee is consistently missing deadlines?

A: I would first meet with the employee to understand the reasons behind the missed deadlines. If there are valid reasons, such as workload or lack of resources, I would work with their manager to address those issues. If the missed deadlines are due to the employee's performance, I would develop a performance improvement plan with specific goals and timelines. I would provide regular feedback and coaching to help the employee improve their performance.

10. Q: An employee requests a salary increase, but their performance does not merit it. How would you handle this situation?

A: I would meet with the employee to discuss their request and understand their perspective. I would then review their performance and compare their salary to market data and internal equity. If their performance does not merit a salary increase, I would explain the reasons why and provide feedback on areas for improvement. I would also discuss alternative ways to recognize their contributions, such as additional responsibilities or professional development opportunities.

11. Q: How would you handle a situation where an employee is not getting along with their team members?

A: I would meet with the employee and their team members separately to understand the root cause of the conflict. I would then facilitate a team meeting to discuss the issues and develop a plan for improving communication and collaboration. If necessary, I would provide training on teamwork and conflict resolution. I would also work with the team manager to monitor progress and provide ongoing support.

12. Q: An employee is consistently not meeting sales targets. How would you address this situation?

A: I would first review the employee's sales performance data and compare it to their targets. I would then meet with the employee and their manager to discuss the reasons behind the missed targets. If there are valid reasons, such as market conditions or lack of leads, I would work with the manager to address those issues. If the missed targets are due to the employee's performance, I would develop a performance improvement plan with specific goals and timelines. I would provide regular coaching and support to help the employee improve their sales skills.

13. Q: How would you handle a situation where an employee is not adhering to the company's dress code?

A: I would first review the company's dress code policy to ensure that it is clear and consistently enforced. I would then meet with the employee to discuss the specific violations and remind them of the policy. If the employee continues to violate the dress code, I would follow the company's disciplinary procedures, which may include verbal warnings, written warnings, and eventually, termination if the behavior does not improve.

14. Q: An employee requests a transfer to another department. How would you handle this request?

A: I would meet with the employee to understand their reasons for requesting a transfer and discuss their career goals. I would then review the employee's qualifications and performance to determine if they are a good fit for the new department. If the transfer is feasible and aligns with the company's needs, I would work with the employee and the new department manager to facilitate the transfer. If the transfer is not possible, I would discuss alternative options with the employee, such as professional development opportunities within their current department.

15. Q: How would you handle a situation where an employee is consistently late in submitting expense reports?

A: I would first review the company's expense reporting policy and procedures to ensure that they are clear and consistently enforced. I would then meet with the employee to discuss the specific violations and remind them of the policy. If the employee continues to submit late expense reports, I would follow the company's disciplinary procedures, which may include verbal warnings, written warnings, and eventually, termination if the behavior does not improve. I would also work with the employee's manager to ensure that they are providing adequate oversight and support.

16. Q: An employee is not meeting the company's expectations for customer service. How would you address this situation?

A: I would first review the company's customer service standards and the employee's performance data. I would then meet with the employee and their manager to discuss the specific issues and develop a plan for improvement. This may include additional training, coaching, and monitoring of the employee's interactions with customers. I would also work with the manager to ensure that they are providing adequate feedback and support to the employee. If the employee's performance does not improve, I would follow the company's disciplinary procedures.

17. Q: How would you handle a situation where an employee is consistently not meeting the company's standards for quality?

A: I would first review the company's quality standards and the employee's performance data. I would then meet with the employee and their manager to discuss the specific issues and develop a plan for improvement. This may include additional training, coaching, and monitoring of the employee's work. I would also work with the manager to ensure that they are providing adequate feedback and support to the employee. If the employee's performance does not improve, I would follow the company's disciplinary procedures.

18. Q: An employee is not adhering to the company's social media policy. How would you address this situation?

A: I would first review the company's social media policy to ensure that it is clear and consistently enforced. I would then meet with the employee to discuss the specific violations and remind them of the policy. If the employee continues to violate the social media policy, I would follow the company's disciplinary procedures, which may include verbal warnings, written warnings, and eventually, termination if the behavior does not improve. I would also work with the employee's manager to ensure that they are providing adequate oversight and guidance on appropriate social media use.

19. Q: How would you handle a situation where an employee is consistently not meeting the company's standards for attendance?

A: I would first review the company's attendance policy and the employee's attendance records. I would then meet with the employee to discuss the specific issues and understand any underlying reasons for the poor attendance. If there are valid reasons, such as medical issues or family emergencies, I would work with the employee to find a solution, such as a flexible work arrangement or leave of absence. If the poor attendance is not justified, I would develop a plan for improvement and follow the company's disciplinary procedures, which may include verbal warnings, written warnings, and eventually, termination if the behavior does not improve.

20. Q: An employee is not maintaining a clean and organized work area. How would you address this situation?

A: I would first review the company's policies on workplace cleanliness and organization. I would then meet with the employee to discuss the specific issues and remind them of the policy. If the employee continues to maintain a messy work area, I would work with their manager to develop a plan for improvement, which may include regular inspections and feedback. If the employee's behavior does not improve, I would follow the company's disciplinary procedures.

21. Q: How would you handle a situation where an employee is consistently not meeting the company's standards for punctuality?

A: I would first review the company's punctuality policy and the employee's attendance records. I would then meet with the employee to discuss the specific issues and understand any underlying reasons for the poor punctuality. If there are valid reasons, such as transportation issues or family obligations, I would work with the employee to find a solution, such as a flexible work schedule or assistance with transportation. If the poor punctuality is not justified, I would develop a plan for improvement and follow the company's disciplinary procedures, which may include verbal warnings, written warnings, and eventually, termination if the behavior does not improve.

22. Q: An employee is consistently not meeting the company's standards for meeting participation. How would you address this situation?

A: I would first review the company's expectations for meeting participation and the employee's performance in meetings. I would then meet with the employee to discuss the specific issues and understand any underlying reasons for the poor participation. If there are valid reasons, such as a lack of confidence or understanding of the subject matter, I would work with the employee to provide training and support. If the poor participation is not justified, I would develop a plan for improvement, which may include setting specific participation goals and providing regular feedback. If the employee's behavior does not improve, I would follow the company's disciplinary procedures.

23. Q: How would you handle a situation where an employee is consistently not responding to emails in a timely manner?

A: I would first review the company's expectations for email responsiveness and the employee's email habits. I would then meet with the employee to discuss the specific issues and understand any underlying reasons for the poor responsiveness. If there are valid reasons, such as a high volume of emails or competing priorities, I would work with the employee to develop strategies for managing their inbox and prioritizing responses. If the poor responsiveness is not justified, I would develop a plan for improvement, which may include setting specific response time goals and providing regular feedback. If the employee's behavior does not improve, I would follow the company's disciplinary procedures.

24. Q: An employee submits a complaint about a coworker's behavior that is not illegal or a violation of company policy, but is still concerning. How would you address this situation?

A: I would take the complaint seriously and meet with the employee to gather more information about the specific behavior and its impact on the workplace. I would then meet with the coworker to discuss the behavior and understand their perspective. If the behavior is inappropriate or disruptive, I would work with the coworker to develop a plan for improvement, which may include training, coaching, or mediation. I would also follow up with the employee who made the complaint to ensure that the situation has been resolved and that they feel comfortable in the workplace.

25. Q: How would you handle a situation where an employee requests a leave of absence for a reason that is not covered by the company's leave policies?

A: I would meet with the employee to understand the specific reason for the leave request and its potential impact on the workplace. I would then review the company's leave policies and consult with upper management to determine if an exception can be made. If the leave request is approved, I would work with the employee and their manager to develop a plan for covering their job duties during their absence and ensuring a smooth transition back to work. If the leave request is denied, I would explain the reasons to the employee and explore alternative options, such as a flexible work arrangement or personal time off.

26. Q: An employee's performance has been consistently excellent, and they request a promotion. How would you handle this request?

A: I would review the employee's job description, performance history, and the company's promotion criteria. I would then meet with the employee's manager to discuss the request and gather their input on the employee's readiness for a promotion. If the employee meets the criteria and there is an available position, I would work with the manager to develop a promotion plan, which may include additional responsibilities, training, and a salary increase. If a promotion is not possible at the time, I would discuss alternative ways to recognize the employee's contributions, such as a bonus, title change, or professional development opportunities.

27. Q: How would you handle a situation where an employee requests a salary increase that is significantly above market rates?

A: I would meet with the employee to understand their perspective and the reasons for the request. I would then review market salary data for similar positions and the company's compensation philosophy. If the request is not justified based on market rates and the employee's performance, I would explain the reasons and discuss alternative ways to recognize their contributions, such as a bonus or additional benefits. If the request is justified, I would work with upper management to determine if a salary increase is feasible and develop a plan for implementing it.

28. Q: An employee is consistently not meeting the company's standards for communication with clients. How would you address this situation?

A: I would first review the company's standards for client communication and the employee's performance in this area. I would then meet with the employee to discuss the specific issues and understand any underlying reasons for the poor communication. If there are valid reasons, such as a lack of training or resources, I would work with the employee's manager to provide the necessary support. If the poor communication is not justified, I would develop a plan for improvement, which may include additional training, coaching, and monitoring of the employee's interactions with clients. If the employee's performance does not improve, I would follow the company's disciplinary procedures.

29. Q: How would you handle a situation where an employee is consistently not meeting the company's standards for collaboration with other departments?

A: I would first review the company's expectations for interdepartmental collaboration and the employee's performance in this area. I would then meet with the employee to discuss the specific issues and understand any underlying reasons for the poor collaboration. If there are valid reasons, such as a lack of understanding of other departments' roles or conflicting priorities, I would work with the employee's manager and other department heads to provide clarity and facilitate communication. If the poor collaboration is not justified, I would develop a plan for improvement, which may include cross-functional training, team-building activities, and setting specific collaboration goals. If the employee's performance does not improve, I would follow the company's disciplinary procedures.

30. Q: An employee requests a transfer to a different location due to personal reasons. How would you handle this request?

A: I would meet with the employee to understand their specific situation and the reasons for the transfer request. I would then review the company's transfer policies and consult with the managers of the current and potential new locations to determine if a transfer is feasible. If a transfer is possible and aligns with the company's needs, I would work with the employee and the managers to develop a transition plan, which may include training, relocation assistance, and a timeline for the move. If a transfer is not possible, I would discuss alternative options with the employee, such as a remote work arrangement or a leave of absence.

31. Q: How would you handle a situation where an employee is consistently not meeting the company's standards for time management?

A: I would first review the company's expectations for time management and the employee's performance in this area. I would then meet with the employee to discuss the specific issues and understand any underlying reasons for the poor time management. If there are valid reasons, such as a heavy workload or lack of resources, I would work with the employee's manager to address those issues and provide support. If the poor time management is not justified, I would develop a plan for improvement, which may include training on prioritization and productivity techniques, setting specific goals and deadlines, and providing regular feedback and coaching. If the employee's performance does not improve, I would follow the company's disciplinary procedures.

32. Q: An employee submits a complaint about a manager's behavior that is concerning but not illegal or a clear violation of company policy. How would you address this situation?

A: I would take the complaint seriously and meet with the employee to gather more information about the specific behavior and its impact on the workplace. I would then meet with the manager to discuss the behavior and understand their perspective. If the behavior is inappropriate or inconsistent with the company's values, I would work with the manager's supervisor to develop a plan for improvement, which may include leadership coaching, training, or disciplinary action. I would also follow up with the employee who made the complaint to ensure that the situation has been resolved and that they feel comfortable in the workplace. If the behavior is found to be illegal or a clear violation of company policy, I would involve upper management and follow the appropriate disciplinary procedures.

33. Q: How would you handle a situation where an employee requests a leave of absence to pursue a personal passion project?

A: I would meet with the employee to understand the nature of the passion project and its potential impact on their work. I would then review the company's leave policies and consult with upper management to determine if an extended leave can be accommodated. If the leave is approved, I would work with the employee and their manager to develop a plan for covering their job duties during their absence, maintaining communication, and ensuring a smooth transition back to work. If the leave is not approved, I would discuss alternative options with the employee, such as a sabbatical program or a flexible work arrangement that allows them to pursue the project while still meeting their job responsibilities.

34. Q: An employee's performance has been consistently poor, despite multiple interventions and improvement plans. How would you handle this situation?

A: I would review the employee's performance history, improvement plans, and documentation of previous interventions. I would then meet with the employee's manager to discuss the situation and determine if termination is warranted. If the decision is made to terminate the employee, I would work with the manager to develop a transition plan, which may include redistributing job duties, hiring a replacement, and communicating the change to the team. I would also ensure that the termination is carried out in compliance with company policies and legal requirements, such as providing notice, severance pay, and benefits information. Throughout the process, I would treat the employee with respect and professionalism.

35. Q: How would you handle a situation where an employee requests a salary increase based on their long tenure with the company, but their performance has been average?

A: I would meet with the employee to acknowledge their long tenure and contributions to the company. I would then review their performance history and market salary data for their position. If their performance has been consistently average and their salary is already in line with market rates, I would explain that a salary increase is not justified at this time. However, I would discuss alternative ways to recognize their loyalty and contributions, such as a one-time bonus, additional vacation days, or opportunities for professional development. I would also encourage the employee to focus on improving their performance and set specific goals for the future.

36. Q: An employee is consistently not meeting the company's standards for maintaining confidentiality of sensitive information. How would you address this situation?

A: I would first review the company's policies and training on confidentiality and the specific instances of the employee's breaches. I would then meet with the employee to discuss the seriousness of the issue and understand any underlying reasons for the breaches. If the breaches were unintentional and due to a lack of understanding, I would provide additional training and resources. If the breaches were intentional or reckless, I would follow the company's disciplinary procedures, which may include termination depending on the severity and frequency of the breaches. I would also work with the employee's manager and IT department to implement safeguards and monitoring to prevent future breaches.

37. Q: How would you handle a situation where an employee is consistently not meeting the company's standards for maintaining a professional appearance?

A: I would first review the company's dress code policy and the specific instances of the employee's violations. I would then meet with the employee to discuss the policy and the importance of maintaining a professional appearance. If there are extenuating circumstances, such as financial hardship or medical issues, I would work with the employee to find a solution, such as providing a clothing allowance or accommodating their needs. If there are no extenuating circumstances, I would provide guidance and resources on appropriate attire and grooming. If the employee continues to violate the policy, I would follow the company's disciplinary procedures, which may include verbal warnings, written warnings, and eventually, termination if the behavior does not improve.

38. Q: An employee submits a complaint about a coworker's personal hygiene that is affecting the work environment. How would you address this situation?

A: I would meet with the employee who submitted the complaint to gather more information about the specific hygiene issues and their impact on the workplace. I would then meet with the coworker in question to discuss the concerns in a sensitive and respectful manner. If there are medical or cultural factors contributing to the hygiene issues, I would work with the coworker to find a solution that accommodates their needs while still maintaining a professional and comfortable work environment for all employees. If there are no extenuating circumstances, I would provide guidance and resources on appropriate hygiene practices and set clear expectations for improvement.

I would also follow up with both employees to ensure that the situation has been resolved and that they feel comfortable in the workplace.

39. Q: How would you handle a situation where an employee requests a transfer to a different department, but their current manager is resistant to the idea?

A: I would meet with the employee to understand their reasons for requesting the transfer and their long-term career goals. I would then meet with their current manager to discuss the request and understand their concerns. If the manager's concerns are valid, such as the employee's critical role in the current department or their lack of qualifications for the new role, I would work with the employee to develop a plan for addressing those concerns, such as cross-training other team members or providing additional training to the employee. If the manager's concerns are not valid, I would advocate for the employee's transfer and work with both managers to develop a transition plan that minimizes disruption to both departments.

40. Q: An employee's performance has been consistently excellent, but they are not interested in taking on additional responsibilities or advancing to a leadership role. How would you handle this situation?

A: I would meet with the employee to acknowledge their excellent performance and understand their career goals and preferences. If they are satisfied in their current role and do not wish to take on additional responsibilities, I would respect their decision and work with their manager to find ways to keep them engaged and motivated, such as providing new challenges within their current role or offering opportunities for lateral moves or special projects. If they are interested in professional development but not leadership, I would work with them to identify training or mentoring opportunities that align with their goals. I would also ensure that their compensation and recognition are commensurate with their performance and contributions to the company.

41. Q: How would you handle a situation where an employee is consistently not meeting the company's standards for maintaining a safe work environment?

A: I would first review the company's safety policies and training, as well as the specific instances of the employee's violations. I would then meet with the employee to discuss the seriousness of the issue and understand any underlying reasons for the violations. If the violations were unintentional and due to a lack of understanding, I would provide additional training and resources. If the violations were intentional or reckless, I would follow the company's disciplinary procedures, which may include termination depending on the severity and frequency of the violations. I would also work with the employee's manager and the safety department to implement additional safety measures and monitoring to prevent future incidents.

42. Q: An employee submits a complaint about a vendor's unprofessional behavior. How would you address this situation?

A: I would meet with the employee to gather more information about the specific behavior and its impact on the business relationship. I would then review the vendor's contract and service level agreements to determine if the behavior constitutes a breach. If it does, I would work with the appropriate departments, such as legal and procurement, to address the issue with the vendor and seek appropriate remedies, such as termination of the contract or financial compensation. If the behavior does not constitute a breach but is still concerning, I would work with the vendor's management to address the issue and set clear expectations for future interactions. I would also follow up with the employee to ensure that the situation has been resolved and that they feel comfortable working with the vendor going forward.

43. Q: How would you handle a situation where an employee requests a leave of absence to care for a sick family member, but their absence would create significant hardship for the department?

A: I would meet with the employee to express empathy for their situation and gather more information about the expected duration and nature of the leave. I would then review the company's leave policies and the employee's eligibility for protected leave under laws such as the Family and Medical Leave Act (FMLA). If the employee is eligible for protected leave, I would work with their manager to develop a coverage plan for their absence, which may include redistributing workload, bringing in temporary staff, or offering overtime to other team members. If the employee is not eligible for protected leave, I would still work with their manager to find a solution that balances the employee's needs with the department's operational requirements, such as a reduced schedule or remote work arrangement. Throughout the process, I would communicate regularly with the employee and their manager to ensure a smooth transition and return to work.

44. Q: An employee's performance has been inconsistent, with periods of excellent work followed by periods of missed deadlines and poor quality. How would you handle this situation?

A: I would meet with the employee to discuss the inconsistency in their performance and understand any underlying reasons, such as personal issues, workload fluctuations, or skill gaps. I would then work with their manager to develop a performance improvement plan that addresses the specific issues and sets clear expectations for consistency. This may include additional training, regular check-ins, or adjustments to their workload or responsibilities. I would also encourage the employee to communicate proactively about any challenges or support they need to maintain consistent performance. If the inconsistency persists despite these interventions, I would follow the company's disciplinary procedures, which may include progressive warnings and eventual termination if the issues are not resolved.

45. Q: How would you handle a situation where an employee is consistently not meeting the company's standards for maintaining accurate records and documentation?

A: I would first review the company's policies and procedures for record-keeping and documentation, as well as the specific instances of the employee's errors or omissions. I would then meet with the employee to discuss the importance of accurate records and understand any underlying reasons for the issues, such as lack of training, time pressure, or unclear expectations. I would provide additional training and resources as needed, and work with the employee's manager to implement quality control measures, such as regular audits or peer review. If the issues persist, I would follow the company's disciplinary procedures, which may include progressive warnings and eventual termination if the employee's performance does not improve.

46. Q: An employee submits a complaint about a customer's inappropriate behavior. How would you address this situation?

A: I would meet with the employee to gather more information about the specific behavior and its impact on the employee and the business relationship. I would then review the company's policies and procedures for handling customer complaints and misconduct. If the behavior constitutes harassment, discrimination, or other illegal conduct, I would involve the appropriate departments, such as legal and security, to investigate and take appropriate action, such as banning the customer from the premises or pursuing legal remedies. If the behavior is inappropriate but not illegal, I would work with the employee's manager and the customer service department to address the issue with the customer and set clear expectations for future interactions. I would also ensure that the employee receives appropriate support and resources, such as counseling or additional training on handling difficult customers.

47. Q: How would you handle a situation where an employee requests a transfer to a different location, but there are no available positions at that location?

A: I would meet with the employee to understand their reasons for requesting the transfer and explore alternative options that may meet their needs, such as remote work, flexible scheduling, or job sharing. I would also review the company's policies and procedures for transfers and explain the criteria and timeline for considering transfer requests. If there are no available positions at the desired location and no alternative options that meet the employee's needs, I would communicate the decision clearly and empathetically, and work with the employee and their manager to address any underlying issues that may have motivated the transfer request, such as job satisfaction or work-life balance. I would also encourage the employee to continue to express their career goals and keep them informed of future opportunities that may align with their interests.

48. Q: An employee's performance has been consistently excellent, and they are being recruited by a competitor. How would you handle this situation?

A: I would meet with the employee to acknowledge their excellent performance and express the company's appreciation for their contributions. I would then seek to understand their reasons for considering the competitor's offer and identify any areas where the company may be able to improve their job satisfaction or career prospects, such as additional compensation, benefits, or development opportunities. I would also review the company's policies and procedures for counter-offers and retention, and work with the employee's manager and upper management to develop a competitive package that aligns with the company's budget and strategic priorities. If the employee ultimately decides to accept the competitor's offer, I would express gratitude for their service and work with their manager to develop a transition plan that minimizes disruption to the team and the business.

49. Q: Q: How would you handle a situation where an employee is consistently not meeting the company's standards for maintaining a positive attitude and demeanor?

A: I would first review the company's policies and expectations for employee conduct and professionalism, as well as the specific instances of the employee's negative attitude or behavior. I would then meet with the employee to discuss the impact of their attitude on the team and the workplace culture, and understand any underlying reasons for the issues, such as personal stress, job dissatisfaction, or interpersonal conflicts. I would provide coaching and resources to help the employee develop a more positive outlook and communication style, such as stress management techniques, assertiveness training, or conflict resolution skills. I would also work with their manager to identify any contributing factors in the work environment, such as unclear expectations, lack of recognition, or toxic team dynamics, and develop a plan to address those issues. If the employee's attitude does not improve despite these interventions, I would follow the company's disciplinary procedures, which may include progressive warnings and eventual termination if the behavior continues to disrupt the team and the business. Throughout the process, I would emphasize the importance of a positive attitude and professionalism in the workplace, and provide ongoing support and feedback to help the employee meet those expectations.

50. Q: An employee submits a complaint about a vendor's breach of confidentiality. How would you address this situation?

A: I would meet with the employee to gather more information about the specific breach and its potential impact on the company's business and reputation. I would then review the vendor's contract and non-disclosure agreements to determine if the breach constitutes a violation of those agreements. If it does, I would work with the appropriate departments, such as legal and IT, to investigate the breach and assess the extent of the damage. Depending on the severity of the breach, I may recommend terminating the vendor's contract, pursuing legal action, or requiring the vendor to take corrective actions, such as improved security measures or employee training. I would also work with the company's PR and communications teams to develop a response plan for any potential media or customer inquiries related to the breach. Throughout the process, I would keep the employee informed of the progress and outcome of the investigation, and ensure that they are protected from any retaliation or further breaches of confidentiality.

51. Q: How would you handle a situation where an employee requests an accommodation for a disability, but the requested accommodation would be very costly for the company?

A: I would meet with the employee to gather more information about their specific needs and the essential functions of their job. I would then review the company's policies and procedures for reasonable accommodations under the Americans with Disabilities Act (ADA) and engage in an interactive process with the employee to identify potential accommodations that would enable them to perform their job duties. If the requested accommodation is very costly, I would explore alternative accommodations that may be more cost-effective while still meeting the employee's needs, such as assistive technology, flexible scheduling, or job restructuring. I would also consult with the company's finance and legal departments to determine the feasibility and legal implications of the various options. If there are no reasonable accommodations that would enable the employee to perform their essential job functions without undue hardship to the company, I would communicate that decision clearly and empathetically, and work with the employee to explore alternative options, such as a transfer to a different position or a leave of absence. Throughout the process, I would maintain confidentiality and treat the employee with respect and sensitivity.

52. Q: An employee's performance has been consistently poor, and they have been placed on a performance improvement plan. However, they are now claiming that the performance issues are due to a previously undisclosed medical condition. How would you handle this situation?

A: I would meet with the employee to gather more information about their medical condition and its impact on their performance. I would then review the company's policies and procedures for accommodating employees with disabilities, as well as the documentation and timeline of the employee's performance issues and improvement plan. If the employee's medical condition qualifies as a disability under the ADA and the performance issues are directly related to that disability, I would engage in an interactive process with the employee to identify reasonable accommodations that may enable them to meet the performance standards, such as additional training, assistive technology, or a modified work schedule. I would also consult with the employee's manager and the company's legal department to ensure that any accommodations are consistent with the company's policies and do not create an undue hardship. If the employee's medical condition does not qualify as a disability or is not directly related to the performance issues, I would continue to hold the employee accountable to the performance improvement plan and provide ongoing feedback and support to help them meet the expectations. Throughout the process, I would maintain confidentiality and treat the employee with respect and empathy, while also balancing the needs of the business and the fairness to other employees.

53. Q: How would you handle a situation where an employee is consistently not meeting the company's standards for maintaining a clean and organized workspace, and their behavior is affecting the productivity and morale of their colleagues?

A: I would first review the company's policies and expectations for workplace organization and cleanliness, as well as the specific instances of the employee's behavior and its impact on their colleagues. I would then meet with the employee to discuss the importance of maintaining a professional and efficient workspace, and understand any underlying reasons for the issues, such as lack of training, time management skills, or personal challenges. I would provide coaching and resources to help the employee develop better organizational habits and time management techniques, such as decluttering, filing systems, or productivity apps. I would also work with their manager to set clear expectations and consequences for non-compliance, such as regular inspections or disciplinary action. If the employee's behavior does not improve despite these interventions, I would follow the company's progressive disciplinary procedures, which may include verbal warnings, written warnings, and eventual termination if the behavior continues to disrupt the team and the business. Throughout the process, I would emphasize the importance of a clean and organized workspace for the employee's own productivity and the respect for their colleagues, and provide ongoing support and feedback to help them meet those expectations.

54. Q: An employee submits a complaint about a customer's discriminatory behavior. How would you address this situation?

A: I would meet with the employee to gather more information about the specific behavior and its impact on the employee and the business relationship. I would then review the company's policies and procedures for handling discrimination complaints and consult with the legal department to determine the appropriate course of action. If the behavior constitutes illegal discrimination, I would work with the appropriate departments, such as legal and HR, to investigate the complaint and take appropriate action, such as terminating the business relationship with the customer or pursuing legal remedies. I would also ensure that the employee receives appropriate support and resources, such as counseling or additional training on handling discriminatory behavior. If the behavior is not illegal but still inappropriate, I would work with the customer service department to address the issue with the customer and set clear expectations for future interactions. Throughout the process, I would communicate regularly with the employee and ensure that they are protected from any retaliation or further discrimination.

55. Q: How would you handle a situation where an employee requests a leave of absence for a personal reason, such as a sabbatical or extended vacation, but their absence would create significant hardship for the department?

A: I would meet with the employee to understand their reasons for requesting the leave and the specific details of their request, such as the duration and timing of the leave. I would then review the company's policies and procedures for personal leaves of absence and consult with the employee's manager to assess the potential impact of their absence on the department's operations and workload. If the department can accommodate the leave without undue hardship, I would work with the employee and their manager to develop a coverage plan and ensure a smooth transition before and after the leave. If the leave would create significant hardship for the department, I would explore alternative options with the employee, such as a shorter leave duration, a different timing, or a combination of paid and unpaid leave. If no reasonable alternative can be found, I would communicate the decision clearly and empathetically to the employee and work with them to find other ways to support their personal goals and well-being, such as additional paid time off, flexible scheduling, or professional development opportunities.

56. Q: An employee's performance has been consistently excellent, and they are being offered a position at another company with a higher salary and more responsibilities. How would you handle this situation?

A: I would meet with the employee to acknowledge their excellent performance and express the company's appreciation for their contributions. I would then seek to understand their reasons for considering the other offer and identify any areas where the company may be able to improve their job satisfaction, compensation, or career prospects. I would review the company's policies and procedures for counter-offers and promotions, and work with the employee's manager and upper management to develop a competitive retention package that aligns with the company's budget and strategic priorities. This may include a salary increase, bonus, additional benefits, or a promotion with expanded responsibilities and growth opportunities. If the company is unable to match the other offer or the employee ultimately decides to accept it, I would express gratitude for their service and work with their manager to develop a transition plan that minimizes disruption to the team and the business. I would also conduct an exit interview to gather feedback on the employee's experience and identify any areas for improvement in the company's retention strategies.

57. Q: How would you handle a situation where an employee is consistently not meeting the company's standards for maintaining confidentiality of customer information, and their behavior is putting the company at risk of a data breach?

A: I would first review the company's policies and procedures for data privacy and security, as well as the specific instances of the employee's behavior and the potential consequences of a data breach. I would then meet with the employee to discuss the severity of the issue and the importance of maintaining the confidentiality of customer information. I would provide additional training and resources on data privacy best practices and the company's security protocols, and work with the IT department to implement additional technical safeguards and monitoring of the employee's access to sensitive data. If the employee's behavior does not improve despite these interventions, I would follow the company's disciplinary procedures for data privacy violations, which may include suspension, termination, and legal action depending on the severity and frequency of the violations. I would also work with the legal and PR departments to develop a response plan for any potential data breaches or customer complaints related to the employee's behavior. Throughout the process, I would emphasize the critical importance of data privacy and security for the trust and loyalty of our customers, and the serious consequences of any breaches or violations. I would continue to monitor the situation closely and be prepared to escalate disciplinary actions if the employee remains unwilling or unable to meet the company's standards for maintaining confidentiality.

58. Q: An employee submits a complaint about a vendor's unethical business practices. How would you address this situation?

A: I would meet with the employee to gather more information about the specific practices and their potential impact on the company's reputation and legal compliance. I would then review the vendor's contract and business agreements to determine if the practices constitute a violation of those agreements or any applicable laws and regulations. If the practices are unethical but not illegal, I would work with the procurement and legal departments to address the issue with the vendor and set clear expectations for ethical conduct in future business dealings. This may include requiring the vendor to implement corrective actions, such as improved training or oversight, or terminating the business relationship if the vendor is unwilling or unable to meet our ethical standards. If the practices are illegal, I would involve the appropriate authorities and cooperate with any investigations or legal proceedings. Throughout the process, I would keep the employee informed of the progress and outcome of the complaint, and ensure that they are protected from any retaliation or negative consequences for raising the issue.

59. Q: How would you handle a situation where an employee requests accommodation for a religious practice, such as time off for a holiday or a prayer room, but the accommodation would be disruptive to the business operations?

A: I would meet with the employee to gather more information about their specific religious needs and the potential impact of the requested accommodation on their job duties and the business operations. I would then review the company's policies and procedures for religious accommodations and engage in an interactive process with the employee to identify potential accommodations that would balance their religious needs with the business requirements. This may include alternative scheduling, voluntary shift swaps, or designated prayer spaces that do not interfere with work areas. If the requested accommodation would pose an undue hardship to the business, such as significant cost, decreased efficiency, or infringement on other employees' rights, I would explore alternative accommodations that may be less disruptive while still respecting the employee's religious beliefs. If no reasonable accommodation can be found, I would communicate the decision clearly and respectfully to the employee and work with them to find other ways to support their religious practices, such as additional unpaid time off or community resources. Throughout the process, I would ensure that the employee is treated with dignity and respect, and that the company's policies are applied consistently and fairly to all employees regardless of their religious beliefs.

60. Q: An employee's performance has been consistently poor, and they have been placed on a performance improvement plan. However, they are now claiming that the performance issues are due to a hostile work environment and discrimination by their manager. How would you handle this situation?

A: I would meet with the employee to gather more information about their specific allegations of hostile work environment and discrimination, and the relationship between those allegations and their performance issues. I would then review the company's policies and procedures for harassment and discrimination complaints, as well as the documentation and timeline of the employee's performance issues and improvement plan. If the employee's allegations are substantiated and the hostile work environment or discrimination is directly related to their performance issues, I would involve the appropriate departments, such as legal and employee relations, to investigate the complaint and take appropriate action, such as disciplinary measures against the manager or changes to the work environment. I would also work with the employee and their new manager to revise the performance improvement plan and provide additional support and resources to help them succeed in their role. If the allegations are not substantiated or are not directly related to the performance issues, I would continue to hold the employee accountable to the performance improvement plan while also addressing any concerns about the work environment or management style. Throughout the process, I would maintain impartiality and confidentiality, and ensure that all parties are treated with respect and fairness in accordance with the company's policies and values.

61. Q: How would you handle a situation where an employee is consistently not meeting the company's standards for maintaining a professional demeanor and language in customer interactions, and their behavior is resulting in customer complaints and lost business?

A: I would first review the company's policies and expectations for customer service and professionalism, as well as the specific instances of the employee's behavior and the impact on customer satisfaction and retention. I would then meet with the employee to discuss the importance of maintaining a professional demeanor and language in all customer interactions, and the consequences of their behavior for the business and their own job performance. I would provide additional training and coaching on customer service best practices, communication skills, and emotional intelligence, and work with their manager to set clear expectations and metrics for improvement. If the employee's behavior does not improve despite these interventions, I would follow the company's disciplinary procedures for customer service violations, which may include verbal warnings, written warnings, and eventual termination if the behavior continues to harm the business and the brand reputation. I would also work with the customer service department to develop a plan for addressing the affected customers and repairing any damaged relationships, such as offering apologies, compensation, or personalized attention. Throughout the process, I would emphasize the critical importance of professionalism and empathy in customer service, and the direct impact of each employee's behavior on the success and growth of the business.

62. Q: An employee submits a complaint about a coworker's inappropriate social media posts that are damaging to the company's reputation. How would you address this situation?

A: I would meet with the employee who submitted the complaint to gather more information about the specific posts and their potential impact on the company's reputation and brand image. I would then review the company's policies and procedures for employee social media conduct and discuss the situation with the coworker in question. If the posts are in violation of company policy or causing significant harm to the business, I would work with the legal and PR departments to determine the appropriate course of action, such as requiring the coworker to remove the posts, issuing a public apology or clarification, or taking disciplinary action against the coworker, up to and including termination. I would also provide training and guidance to all employees on responsible social media use and the potential consequences of inappropriate posts for both the individual and the company. Throughout the process, I would maintain confidentiality and professionalism, and ensure that all parties are treated fairly and consistently in accordance with the company's policies and values.

63. Q: How would you handle a situation where an employee requests a leave of absence for a mental health condition, but they are reluctant to disclose the details of their condition to their manager or colleagues?

A: I would meet with the employee to discuss their leave request and assure them of the confidentiality of their medical information. I would then review the company's policies and procedures for medical leaves of absence and the employee's eligibility for protected leave under laws such as the Family and Medical Leave Act (FMLA) and the Americans with Disabilities Act (ADA). If the employee is eligible for protected leave, I would work with them to obtain the necessary medical certification and documentation, and develop a plan for their absence and return to work that maintains their privacy and dignity. I would also educate the employee's manager and colleagues on the importance of respecting the employee's privacy and not speculating or gossiping about their condition or leave. If the employee is not eligible for protected leave or chooses not to disclose their condition, I would still work with them to find a solution that balances their mental health needs with the business requirements, such as a reduced schedule, temporary reassignment, or employee assistance program (EAP) resources. Throughout the process, I would emphasize the company's commitment to supporting the health and well-being of all employees, and the availability of confidential resources and accommodations for mental health conditions.

64. Q: An employee's performance has been consistently excellent, but they are now exhibiting signs of burnout and stress. How would you handle this situation?

A: I would meet with the employee to express concern for their well-being and gather more information about the factors contributing to their burnout and stress, such as workload, work-life balance, or interpersonal conflicts. I would then work with the employee and their manager to develop a plan for addressing those factors and supporting the employee's resilience and job satisfaction. This may include adjusting their workload or responsibilities, providing additional resources or support staff, encouraging the use of paid time off and wellness benefits, or facilitating conflict resolution or team-building activities. I would also educate the employee and their colleagues on the signs and risks of burnout, and the importance of self-care, stress management, and open communication. If the employee's condition is severe or not improving with these interventions, I would recommend a referral to the employee assistance program (EAP) or a leave of absence to allow for rest and recovery. Throughout the process, I would emphasize the company's commitment to the health and well-being of all employees, and the value of preventing and addressing burnout for both individual and organizational success.

65. Q: How would you handle a situation where an employee is consistently not meeting the company's standards for maintaining accurate and timely records, and their behavior is resulting in errors and delays in billing and financial reporting?

A: I would first review the company's policies and procedures for record-keeping and documentation, as well as the specific instances of the employee's errors and delays and the impact on the business operations. I would then meet with the employee to discuss the importance of accurate and timely records for the company's financial health and compliance, and the consequences of their behavior for their own job performance and the team's productivity. I would provide additional training and resources on record-keeping best practices, time management, and attention to detail, and work with their manager to set clear expectations and metrics for improvement. If the employee's behavior does not improve despite these interventions, I would follow the company's disciplinary procedures for performance issues, which may include verbal warnings, written warnings, and eventual termination if the errors and delays continue to harm the business and the team. I would also work with the finance and accounting departments to develop a plan for identifying and correcting any past errors or discrepancies, and implementing additional quality control measures and oversight to prevent future issues. Throughout the process, I would emphasize the critical importance of accuracy and timeliness in financial record-keeping, and the responsibility of each employee to maintain the highest standards of integrity and professionalism in their work.

66. Q: An employee submits a complaint about a customer's sexual harassment of them during a business interaction. How would you address this situation?

A: I would meet with the employee to express support and empathy for their experience, and gather more information about the specific incident and any previous incidents or patterns of harassment by the customer. I would then review the company's policies and procedures for addressing sexual harassment complaints and discuss the employee's options for reporting and resolving the situation, such as filing a formal complaint, involving law enforcement, or seeking a restraining order. I would also take immediate action to protect the employee from further harassment, such as reassigning them to a different account or location, or terminating the business relationship with the customer if the harassment is severe or persistent. I would provide the employee with resources and support, such as counseling, legal assistance, or time off, and ensure that they are not retaliated against or disadvantaged for reporting the harassment. I would also work with the company's legal and HR departments to investigate the complaint, document the findings, and take appropriate disciplinary action against the customer or any employees who enabled or failed to prevent the harassment. Throughout the process, I would prioritize the safety, dignity, and well-being of the employee, and send a clear message that sexual harassment is never acceptable or tolerated in our business.

67. Q: How would you handle a situation where an employee requests accommodation for a medical condition that requires frequent breaks and time off

for treatment, but their absence is causing staffing shortages and decreased productivity in their department?

A: I would meet with the employee to discuss their accommodation request and gather more information about their specific medical needs and the potential impact on their job duties and the department's operations. I would then review the company's policies and procedures for medical accommodations and engage in an interactive process with the employee and their manager to identify potential accommodations that would balance the employee's health needs with the business requirements. This may include a modified work schedule, temporary reassignment of duties, or the use of intermittent FMLA leave for treatment. If the employee's condition is expected to be long-term or permanent, I would also explore the possibility of reassigning them to a different position or department that can better accommodate their needs. If the accommodation would pose an undue hardship to the business, such as significant loss of productivity or the inability to meet customer demands, I would document the reasons and explore alternative accommodations that may be less disruptive. Throughout the process, I would maintain open and respectful communication with the employee and their manager, and ensure that the employee's medical information is kept confidential and separate from their personnel file. I would also work with the department to develop a plan for managing the staffing shortages and workload, such as hiring temporary staff, cross-training other employees, or adjusting deadlines and expectations. The goal would be to find a solution that allows the employee to manage their health while also maintaining the department's ability to meet its goals and serve its customers.

68. Q: An employee's performance has been consistently poor, and they have been placed on a performance improvement plan. However, they are now claiming that the performance issues are due to a personal crisis, such as a divorce or family illness, and they are requesting more time and leniency to improve. How would you handle this situation?

A: I would meet with the employee to express empathy for their personal situation and gather more information about the specific challenges they are facing and the impact on their work performance. I would then review the company's policies and procedures for performance management and personal leave, as well as the documentation and timeline of the employee's performance issues and improvement plan. If the employee's personal crisis is temporary and not expected to have a long-term impact on their ability to perform their job duties, I would work with them and their manager to adjust the performance improvement plan and provide additional support and resources, such as EAP counseling, flexible scheduling, or short-term leave. I would also set clear expectations for communication and accountability during this time, such as regular check-ins and progress reports. If the employee's personal crisis is severe or expected to have a long-term impact on their performance, I would explore the possibility of a longer leave of absence or a temporary reassignment to a different role or department that can better accommodate their needs. If the employee is unable or unwilling to improve their performance even with these accommodations, I would follow the company's disciplinary procedures for performance issues, which may include termination if the business needs cannot be met. Throughout the process, I would maintain confidentiality and professionalism, and ensure that the employee is treated with compassion and respect while also holding them accountable for meeting the essential functions of their job.

69. Q: How would you handle a situation where an employee is consistently not meeting the company's standards for maintaining a safe and secure work environment, such as not following proper safety protocols or leaving confidential information unsecured, and their behavior is putting themselves and others at risk?

A: I would first review the company's policies and procedures for workplace safety and security, as well as the specific instances of the employee's violations and the potential risks and liabilities for the business. I would then meet with the employee to discuss the seriousness of the issue and the importance of following all safety and security protocols, not only for their own protection but also for the well-being of their colleagues and the company as a whole. I would provide additional training and resources on the specific protocols and best practices, and work with their manager to implement a system of regular audits and inspections to ensure compliance. If the employee's behavior does not improve despite these interventions, I would follow the company's disciplinary procedures for safety and security violations, which may include verbal warnings, written warnings, suspension, and eventual termination if the violations continue to put people and assets at risk. I would also work with the facilities and IT departments to identify and address any systemic issues or vulnerabilities that may be contributing to the problem, such as inadequate safety equipment, outdated security software, or lack of employee awareness and engagement. Throughout the process, I would emphasize the critical importance of safety and security in the workplace, and the responsibility of each employee to be vigilant and proactive in protecting themselves, their colleagues, and the company's resources and reputation.

70. Q: An employee submits a complaint about a vendor's failure to deliver products or services as promised, resulting in delays and additional costs for the company. How would you address this situation?

A: I would meet with the employee to gather more information about the specific issues with the vendor's performance and the impact on the company's operations and bottom line. I would then review the vendor's contract and service level agreements to determine if the issues constitute a breach of contract or a failure to meet the agreed-upon terms and conditions. If the issues are significant and well-documented, I would work with the procurement and legal departments to address the situation with the vendor, either through a formal dispute resolution process or by terminating the contract and seeking damages. I would also work with the affected departments to develop a contingency plan for sourcing alternative products or services and minimizing the impact on the business. If the issues are minor or isolated incidents, I would still address them with the vendor and seek corrective action and assurances of future performance. Throughout the process, I would keep the employee and other stakeholders informed of the progress and outcome of the complaint, and ensure that the company's interests are protected and the vendor is held accountable for their obligations. I would also use the experience to review and improve the company's vendor selection and management processes, such as conducting more thorough due diligence, setting clearer performance metrics and penalties, and maintaining open and proactive communication with vendors to identify and resolve issues early.

71. Q: How would you handle a situation where an employee requests a transfer to a different department or location due to conflicts with their coworkers or manager, but there are no available openings or the employee's skills and experience are not a good fit for the desired role?

A: I would meet with the employee to discuss their reasons for requesting the transfer and gather more information about the specific conflicts or issues they are experiencing in their current role. I would then review the company's policies and procedures for internal transfers and career development, as well as the job descriptions and requirements for the desired role or location. If the employee's skills and experience are not a good fit for the desired role, or if there are no available openings, I would explain the reasons and explore alternative options for addressing the underlying conflicts or issues. This may include mediation or conflict resolution with the coworkers or manager, additional training or support for the employee to improve their communication and collaboration skills, or a temporary reassignment or project to provide a change of pace or environment. If the conflicts are severe or not resolvable through these interventions, I would work with the employee and their manager to develop a longer-term career development plan that aligns with their strengths and interests and the company's needs and opportunities. This may include identifying potential future openings or creating a new role that leverages the employee's unique skills and experience.

Throughout the process, I would maintain open and honest communication with the employee about the feasibility and timeline of their transfer request, and provide ongoing support and guidance to help them navigate their career path and maintain their engagement and productivity in their current role.

72. Q: An employee's performance has been consistently excellent, but they are now facing personal challenges, such as a serious illness or family emergency, that are impacting their ability to maintain their previous level of performance. How would you handle this situation?

A: I would meet with the employee to express concern and support for their personal situation, and gather more information about the specific challenges they are facing and the potential impact on their work performance and well-being. I would then review the company's policies and benefits for employees facing personal hardships, such as FMLA leave, short-term disability, employee assistance programs, and flexible work arrangements. I would work with the employee and their manager to develop a plan that balances the employee's need for time off or accommodations with the business needs and the employee's long-term career goals. This may include a reduced schedule, remote work, or a temporary reassignment of duties to other team members. I would also ensure that the employee is aware of and able to access all available resources and support services, such as counseling, financial planning, and community resources. Throughout the process, I would maintain regular communication with the employee and their manager to monitor their well-being and performance, and make adjustments to the plan as needed. I would also ensure that the employee's personal information is kept confidential and that they are not penalized or discriminated against for their personal challenges. The goal would be to support the employee through a difficult time while also ensuring that the business can continue to operate effectively and meet its goals.

73. Q: How would you handle a situation where an employee is consistently not meeting the company's standards for maintaining a professional appearance, such as dress code violations or poor personal hygiene, and their appearance is negatively impacting the company's image and customer relationships?

A: I would first review the company's policies and guidelines for professional appearance and dress code, as well as the specific instances of the employee's violations and the feedback from customers or colleagues. I would then meet with the employee to discuss the importance of maintaining a professional appearance and the impact of their appearance on the company's brand and reputation. I would provide clear guidance and examples of appropriate attire and grooming, and work with the employee to identify any barriers or challenges they may be facing, such as financial constraints or cultural differences. If the employee's appearance is related to a medical condition or disability, I would engage in an interactive process to identify reasonable accommodations, such as modified dress code or grooming standards. If the employee's appearance is not related to a protected status, I would set clear expectations and timelines for improvement, and provide resources such as a clothing allowance or referrals to local clothing banks or personal care services. If the employee's appearance does not improve despite these interventions, I would follow the company's disciplinary procedures for dress code violations, which may include verbal warnings, written warnings, and eventual termination if the violations continue to harm the business and the team. Throughout the process, I would maintain a respectful and non-judgmental approach, and focus on the specific behaviors and standards rather than personal attributes or preferences. I would also ensure that the dress code and appearance policies are applied consistently and fairly to all employees, and that they do not discriminate against any protected classes or individual differences.

74. Q: An employee submits a complaint about a customer's inappropriate behavior, such as making offensive jokes or comments, but the customer is a high-value client for the company. How would you address this situation?

A: I would meet with the employee to gather more information about the specific behavior and comments, and express support and appreciation for their willingness to report the issue. I would then review the company's policies and values around respect, inclusion, and customer service, as well as any relevant laws or regulations. Regardless of the customer's value to the company, I would make it clear that inappropriate or offensive behavior is never acceptable or tolerated, and that the employee's well-being and dignity are a top priority. I would then discuss the situation with the appropriate leaders and stakeholders, such as the account manager, sales director, and legal counsel, to determine the best course of action. This may include directly addressing the behavior with the customer and setting clear expectations and consequences for future interactions, such as requiring the customer to work with a different representative or term inating the business relationship if the behavior persists. I would also provide support and resources to the employee, such as counseling or reassignment to a different account, and ensure that they are not retaliated against or disadvantaged for reporting the issue. Throughout the process, I would maintain open and transparent communication with the employee and the customer, and seek to find a resolution that upholds the company's values and standards while also preserving important business relationships if possible. I would also use the situation as an opportunity to review and reinforce the company's policies and training on harassment, discrimination, and customer service, and ensure that all employees feel empowered and supported to speak up about inappropriate behavior from any source.

75. Q: How would you handle a situation where an employee requests accommodation for a disability that requires significant modifications to their work environment or equipment, but the company has limited budget and resources to make the necessary changes?

A: I would meet with the employee to discuss their specific accommodation needs and gather any necessary medical documentation or recommendations from their healthcare provider. I would then review the company's policies and budget for accommodations, as well as any legal requirements under the ADA or other relevant laws. If the requested accommodations are reasonable and necessary for the employee to perform the essential functions of their job, I would work with the employee, their manager, and the facilities or IT department to identify the most cost-effective and feasible solutions. This may include researching and obtaining funding or grants for assistive technology or equipment, or exploring alternative accommodations that achieve the same goal with less extensive modifications. If the requested accommodations would pose an undue hardship on the company, I would engage in an interactive process with the employee to identify alternative accommodations that balance their needs with the company's resources and constraints. Throughout the process, I would maintain open and collaborative communication with the employee and the relevant stakeholders, and ensure that the employee's privacy and dignity are respected. I would also use the situation as an opportunity to review and improve the company's overall accessibility and inclusion practices, and advocate for additional budget and resources to support a diverse and equitable workplace.

76. Q: An employee's performance has been consistently poor, and they have been placed on a performance improvement plan. However, they are now claiming that the performance issues are due to a lack of training and support from their manager and the company. How would you handle this situation?

A: I would meet with the employee to discuss their concerns and gather more information about the specific areas where they feel they have not received adequate training or support. I would then review the employee's onboarding and development history, as well as the documentation and timeline of their performance issues and improvement plan. If there are gaps or deficiencies in the employee's training or support, I would work with their manager and the HR or learning and development team to identify and provide the necessary resources and guidance. This may include additional training sessions, job shadowing, mentoring, or regular feedback and coaching sessions with their manager. I would also review and clarify the expectations and metrics for the employee's performance, and ensure that they have the tools and information needed to meet those standards. If the employee's performance issues are not solely due to a lack of training or support, I would continue to hold them accountable to the improvement plan and provide ongoing feedback and development opportunities. If the employee's performance does not improve even with the additional support and resources, I would follow the company's disciplinary procedures, which may include termination. Throughout the process, I would maintain a fair and objective approach, and ensure that the employee's feedback and concerns are heard and addressed, while also upholding the company's performance standards and business needs.

77. Q: How would you handle a situation where an employee is consistently not meeting the company's standards for maintaining confidentiality of sensitive information, such as discussing client details in public areas or sharing login credentials with coworkers, and their behavior is putting the company at risk of legal or reputational damage?

A: I would first review the company's policies and training on confidentiality and data privacy, as well as the specific instances of the employee's violations and the potential risks and consequences for the business. I would then meet with the employee to discuss the seriousness of the issue and the importance of maintaining strict confidentiality of sensitive information, both for the protection of the company and its clients and for the employee's own professional responsibility and reputation. I would provide additional training and resources on best practices for handling confidential information, such as using secure communication channels, locking devices when not in use, and reporting any suspicious or unauthorized access. I would also work with the IT and legal departments to implement additional technical and administrative safeguards, such as access controls, encryption, and monitoring of user activity. If the employee's behavior does not improve despite these interventions, I would follow the company's disciplinary procedures for confidentiality breaches, which may include verbal warnings, written warnings, suspension, and eventual termination if the violations continue to put the company at risk. In cases of severe or intentional breaches, I would also involve legal counsel and potentially law enforcement to investigate and pursue any necessary legal action. Throughout the process, I would emphasize the critical importance of confidentiality and data privacy in today's business environment, and the responsibility of each employee to uphold the highest standards of integrity and professionalism in handling sensitive information.

78. Q: An employee submits a complaint about a vendor's unethical business practices, such as using substandard materials or exploiting workers, but the

vendor is the only supplier of a critical component for the company's products. How would you address this situation?

A: I would meet with the employee to gather more information about the specific unethical practices and the evidence or sources supporting the complaint. I would then review the vendor's contract and any relevant industry standards or regulations to determine if the practices violate any legal or contractual obligations. Regardless of the vendor's importance to the company, I would take the complaint seriously and investigate the allegations thoroughly, either through internal audits or third-party assessments. If the unethical practices are confirmed, I would work with the procurement, legal, and executive teams to address the situation with the vendor and explore alternative options. This may include requiring the vendor to implement corrective actions and provide evidence of compliance, or terminating the contract and seeking alternative suppliers, even if it results in short-term disruptions or costs for the company. I would also ensure that the company's own supply chain and procurement practices are reviewed and strengthened to prevent future incidents and align with the company's values and ethical standards. Throughout the process, I would keep the employee and other stakeholders informed of the progress and outcome of the complaint, and ensure that the company's response is transparent and accountable. I would also use the situation as an opportunity to reinforce the company's commitment to ethical and sustainable business practices, and engage employees and partners in ongoing dialogue and education around these issues.

79. Q: How would you handle a situation where an employee requests a leave of absence to pursue a personal development opportunity, such as a sabbatical or volunteer project, but the timing of the leave would be disruptive to the team's workload and objectives?

A: I would meet with the employee to discuss their personal development goals and the specific opportunity they are pursuing, and gather more information about the timing, duration, and impact of the proposed leave. I would then review the company's policies and procedures for personal leaves and sabbaticals, as well as the team's workload and objectives for the relevant time period. If the leave would be significantly disruptive to the team's ability to meet its goals and serve its customers, I would work with the employee and their manager to explore alternative options that balance the employee's personal development with the business needs. This may include adjusting the timing or duration of the leave, finding a way to integrate the development opportunity with the employee's regular work responsibilities, or identifying alternative opportunities that align with the team's schedule and objectives. If a mutually agreeable solution cannot be found, I would clearly communicate the reasons and constraints to the employee, and work with them to find other ways to support their personal development within the context of their job and the company's resources. This may include providing financial support or time off for shorter-term learning opportunities, or creating a long-term development plan that aligns with the employee's career goals and the company's strategic priorities. Throughout the process, I would maintain a supportive and solutions-oriented approach, and ensure that the employee feels heard and valued, even if their specific request cannot be accommodated.

80. Q: An employee's performance has been consistently excellent, but they are now exhibiting signs of disengagement and dissatisfaction with their role and the company. How would you handle this situation?

A: I would meet with the employee to express appreciation for their contributions and performance, and gather more information about the specific factors contributing to their disengagement and dissatisfaction. This may include a lack of challenge or growth in their current role, a misalignment with their personal values or career goals, or concerns about the company's direction or leadership. I would then work with the employee and their manager to develop a plan for addressing those factors and re-engaging the employee in their work and the organization. This may include providing new challenges or responsibilities within their current role, exploring opportunities for lateral moves or promotions that align with their interests and skills, or involving them in strategic projects or initiatives that contribute to the company's mission and vision. I would also ensure that the employee has regular opportunities for feedback, recognition, and development, and that their concerns and ideas are heard and addressed by leadership. If the employee's dissatisfaction is related to broader issues within the company culture or management, I would work with the appropriate stakeholders to identify and address those issues, and involve the employee in the process of positive change. If the employee ultimately decides to leave the company despite these efforts, I would conduct an exit interview to gather insights and feedback, and ensure a smooth and respectful transition for both the employee and the team. Throughout the process, I would maintain open and empathetic communication with the employee, and prioritize their well-being and engagement as a key driver of individual and organizational success.

81. Q: How would you handle a situation where an employee is consistently not meeting the company's standards for maintaining a respectful and inclusive work environment, such as making insensitive comments or jokes, and their behavior is causing discomfort and tension among their colleagues?

A: I would first review the company's policies and training on diversity, equity, and inclusion, as well as the specific instances of the employee's behavior and the impact on their colleagues. I would then meet with the employee to discuss the concerns and the importance of maintaining a respectful and inclusive work environment for all employees, regardless of their personal beliefs or backgrounds. I would provide specific examples of the problematic behavior and explain how it violates the company's values and standards, and potentially legal protections against harassment and discrimination. I would also give the employee an opportunity to share their perspective and any underlying factors contributing to their behavior, such as a lack of awareness or cultural differences. Based on this discussion, I would work with the employee to develop a plan for improving their communication and interpersonal skills, which may include additional training, coaching, or mentoring. I would also set clear expectations and consequences for future behavior, and ensure that the employee understands the seriousness of the issue and the potential disciplinary actions if the behavior persists. In parallel, I would work with the rest of the team and the organization to reinforce the company's commitment to diversity, equity, and inclusion, and provide resources and support for employees who may have been impacted by the behavior. This may include facilitating open dialogues, providing access to employee resource groups or outside experts, and ensuring that all employees feel safe and empowered to report any concerns or incidents. Throughout the process, I would maintain a firm but fair approach, and prioritize the well-being and inclusion of all employees, while also recognizing the potential for growth and change in the individual exhibiting the problematic behavior.

82. Q: An employee submits a complaint about a customer's breach of contract, such as failing to pay for services rendered or violating the terms of use, but the customer is a long-standing and influential client for the company. How would you address this situation?

A: I would meet with the employee to gather more information about the specific breach of contract and the evidence supporting the complaint, such as unpaid invoices, communication records, or usage data. I would then review the customer's contract and any relevant laws or regulations to determine the legal and financial implications of the breach. Regardless of the customer's history or importance to the company, I would take the complaint seriously and investigate the situation objectively and thoroughly. I would then discuss the findings with the appropriate stakeholders, such as the account manager, finance director, and legal counsel, to determine the best course of action. This may include directly addressing the breach with the customer and seeking to resolve the issue through negotiation or mediation, or potentially pursuing legal action if the breach is severe or repeated. I would also work with the relevant teams to assess the potential risks and impacts of the different options, such as the loss of future business, reputational damage, or precedent-setting for other clients. Throughout the process, I would keep the employee and other stakeholders informed of the progress and outcome of the complaint, and ensure that the company's response is consistent, fair, and aligned with its contractual obligations and ethical standards. I would also use the situation as an opportunity to review and strengthen the company's contract management and client communication practices, and ensure that all employees feel supported and empowered to raise concerns about any breaches or violations, regardless of the client's status or relationship with the company.

83. Q: How would you handle a situation where an employee requests accommodation for a mental health condition, such as flexible scheduling or remote work, but their manager is resistant to the idea and concerned about the impact on team productivity and morale?

A: I would meet with the employee to discuss their specific accommodation request and gather any necessary medical documentation or recommendations from their healthcare provider. I would then review the company's policies and legal obligations for accommodating employees with disabilities, including mental health conditions. If the requested accommodation is reasonable and necessary for the employee to perform the essential functions of their job, I would work with the employee, their manager, and any other relevant stakeholders to develop a plan for implementing the accommodation in a way that balances the employee's needs with the team's operational requirements and the manager's concerns. This may include setting clear expectations and communication protocols for flexible scheduling or remote work, identifying alternative accommodations that achieve the same goal, or providing additional resources and support for the employee and the team to ensure a smooth transition. I would also provide education and training for the manager and the team on mental health awareness, stigma reduction, and inclusive management practices, to help create a more supportive and understanding work environment. If the manager's resistance persists or creates a hostile or discriminatory environment for the employee, I would address the behavior directly and take appropriate disciplinary action, up to and including termination, to ensure compliance with the company's policies and legal obligations. Throughout the process, I would maintain open and confidential communication with the employee and ensure that their privacy and dignity are respected, while also working to build a culture of empathy, flexibility, and inclusion that supports the well-being and productivity of all employees.

84. Q: An employee's performance has been consistently poor, and they have been placed on a performance improvement plan. However, they are now claiming that the performance issues are due to a conflict with a coworker who is creating a

hostile work environment, and they are requesting a transfer to a different team. How would you handle this situation?

A: I would meet with the employee to gather more information about the specific conflict with their coworker and the alleged hostile work environment, including any incidents, witnesses, or documentation. I would then review the employee's performance history and improvement plan, as well as any previous complaints or investigations related to the coworker or the team dynamics. If the employee's claims of a hostile work environment are substantiated and appear to be a significant factor in their performance issues, I would involve the appropriate parties, such as the coworker, the manager, and HR, to address the situation and find a resolution. This may include mediation, training, or disciplinary action for the coworker, depending on the severity and frequency of their behavior. I would also consider the employee's request for a transfer and assess the feasibility and appropriateness of such a move, based on the available positions, the employee's skills and qualifications, and the potential impact on both teams. If a transfer is not possible or advisable, I would work with the employee, their manager, and the rest of the team to develop a plan for improving the work environment and the employee's performance, which may include additional support, resources, or accommodations. If the employee's performance issues persist despite the resolution of the hostile work environment, I would continue to hold them accountable to the improvement plan and take appropriate disciplinary action, up to and including termination, if they fail to meet the agreed-upon goals and expectations. Throughout the process, I would maintain impartiality, confidentiality, and adherence to the company's policies and legal obligations, while also prioritizing the safety, well-being, and productivity of all employees involved.

85. Q: How would you handle a situation where an employee is consistently not meeting the company's standards for maintaining accurate and complete personnel records, such as not submitting timesheets or expense reports on time, and their behavior is causing delays and errors in payroll and reimbursements for themselves and their colleagues?

A: I would first review the company's policies and procedures for personnel record-keeping, as well as the specific instances of the employee's errors and omissions and the impact on the payroll and reimbursement processes. I would then meet with the employee to discuss the importance of accurate and timely record-keeping, not only for their own compensation and benefits but also for the efficiency and compliance of the company's financial operations. I would provide additional training and resources on the relevant systems and procedures, and work with the employee's manager to implement regular reminders and check-ins to ensure adherence. If the employee's behavior does not improve despite these interventions, I would follow the company's disciplinary procedures for performance issues, which may include verbal warnings, written warnings, and eventual termination if the errors and delays continue to disrupt the payroll and reimbursement processes. In parallel, I would work with the payroll and accounting teams to identify and correct any past errors or discrepancies caused by the employee's behavior, and implement additional controls and audits to prevent future issues. This may include automating certain processes, requiring manager approval for submissions, or conducting regular reconciliations and spot checks. Throughout the process, I would emphasize the critical importance of accurate and timely record-keeping for the financial integrity and legal compliance of the company, and the responsibility of each employee to adhere to the established policies and procedures. I would also ensure that any disciplinary actions are consistent, fair, and well-documented, and that the employee's confidentiality and due process rights are respected.

86. Q: An employee submits a complaint about a coworker's inappropriate behavior outside of work, such as posting offensive content on social media or engaging in criminal activity, and they are concerned about the potential impact on the company's reputation and their own safety and well-being. How would you address this situation?

A: I would meet with the employee to gather more information about the specific behavior and their concerns, and express appreciation for their willingness to come forward. I would then review the company's policies and codes of conduct regarding off-duty behavior and social media use, as well as any relevant laws or regulations. Depending on the nature and severity of the behavior, I may also involve legal counsel or law enforcement to assess the potential risks and liabilities for the company and the individuals involved. If the behavior violates company policy or raises significant concerns about the coworker's judgment, character, or ability to perform their job duties, I would address the situation directly with the coworker and take appropriate disciplinary action, up to and including termination. This may involve conducting an investigation, gathering evidence, and providing due process and opportunities for the coworker to respond and appeal. Throughout the process, I would prioritize the safety, privacy, and well-being of the reporting employee and any other affected parties, and provide them with resources and support, such as counseling, security measures, or accommodations to minimize their contact with the coworker. I would also communicate with the rest of the organization as needed to address any concerns or rumors, while maintaining confidentiality and professionalism. Ultimately, I would use the situation as an opportunity to reinforce the company's values, expectations, and commitment to a safe, ethical, and respectful workplace culture, and provide training and resources to help prevent and address similar issues in the future.

87. Q: How would you handle a situation where an employee requests accommodation for a religious practice that conflicts with the company's dress code policy, such as wearing a head covering or facial hair, and their manager is concerned about the impact on the company's professional image and customer perceptions?

A: I would meet with the employee to discuss their specific religious accommodation request and gather any necessary documentation or information about the religious practice and its requirements. I would then review the company's dress code policy and any relevant laws or regulations regarding religious accommodations in the workplace. If the requested accommodation does not pose an undue hardship on the company's operations or create a safety hazard, I would work with the employee, their manager, and any other relevant stakeholders to find a mutually acceptable solution that balances the employee's religious needs with the company's business interests. This may involve modifying the dress code policy to allow for religious attire, providing alternative assignments or positions that do not require the same dress standards, or educating customers and colleagues about the diversity and inclusion of different religious practices. If the manager's concerns about professional image or customer perceptions are based on stereotypes or prejudices rather than legitimate business reasons, I would address those biases directly and provide training and resources on religious diversity and non-discrimination. Throughout the process, I would maintain respect for the employee's religious beliefs and practices, and ensure that they are not subjected to any form of harassment, retaliation, or unequal treatment based on their request for accommodation. I would also use the situation as an opportunity to review and update the company's policies and practices around religious accommodations and diversity, and foster a culture of inclusion and respect for all employees, regardless of their religious or cultural background.

88. Q: An employee's performance has been consistently excellent, but they are now facing personal challenges, such as a divorce or substance abuse issue, that are beginning to impact their work attendance and quality. How would you handle this situation?

A: I would meet with the employee to express concern for their well-being and offer support, while also addressing the observed changes in their attendance and performance. I would approach the conversation with empathy, non-judgment, and confidentiality, and create a safe space for the employee to share any relevant information about their personal situation and its impact on their work. Depending on the nature and severity of the personal challenges, I would provide the employee with information and referrals to appropriate resources, such as the Employee Assistance Program (EAP), counseling services, or substance abuse treatment programs. I would also work with the employee and their manager to develop a plan for managing their workload and responsibilities during this time, which may include temporary accommodations, such as flexible scheduling, reduced hours, or a leave of absence. If the employee's performance or attendance issues persist or worsen despite these supportive measures, I would follow the company's standard performance management and disciplinary procedures, while continuing to offer resources and accommodations as appropriate. This may involve setting clear expectations and timelines for improvement, providing regular feedback and coaching, and ultimately, taking disciplinary action up to and including termination if the employee is unable to meet the essential functions of their job. Throughout the process, I would maintain the employee's privacy and dignity, and ensure that any performance or disciplinary actions are based on objective, job-related criteria and not on the employee's personal circumstances or protected characteristics. I would also work with the rest of the organization to create a supportive and inclusive culture that encourages employees to seek help and resources when facing personal challenges, without fear of stigma, discrimination, or retaliation.

89. Q: How would you handle a situation where an employee is consistently not meeting the company's standards for maintaining a positive and collaborative team environment, such as not participating in team meetings or events, and their behavior is causing frustration and resentment among their colleagues?

A: I would first review the company's expectations and norms for team participation and collaboration, as well as the specific instances of the employee's behavior and its impact on team dynamics and morale. I would then meet with the employee to discuss the concerns and understand their perspective and any underlying reasons for their lack of engagement, such as a lack of clarity around their role, a mismatch with their skills or interests, or interpersonal conflicts with teammates. Based on this conversation, I would work with the employee and their manager to develop a plan for improving their participation and collaboration, which may include setting clear expectations and goals, providing additional training or resources, or facilitating team-building activities or discussions to address any conflicts or misunderstandings. I would also encourage the employee to take an active role in shaping the team culture and norms, and to provide feedback and suggestions for how to make the team more inclusive and effective. If the employee's behavior does not improve despite these interventions, I would follow the company's disciplinary procedures for performance issues, which may include verbal warnings, written warnings, and eventual termination if the lack of collaboration continues to negatively impact the team and the business. Throughout the process, I would emphasize the importance of teamwork, communication, and mutual respect in achieving individual and organizational goals, and provide ongoing support and coaching to help the employee develop their collaboration skills and mindset.

90. Q: An employee submits a complaint about a vendor's products or services, such as defects, delays, or poor quality, and they are concerned about the potential impact on the company's operations and customer satisfaction. How would you address this situation?

A: I would meet with the employee to gather more information about the specific issues with the vendor's products or services, including any evidence, examples, or customer feedback. I would then review the vendor's contract, service level agreements, and quality standards to determine if the issues constitute a breach or violation of the agreed-upon terms. If the issues are significant or recurring, I would escalate the complaint to the appropriate stakeholders, such as the procurement, quality, or operations teams, and work with them to address the situation with the vendor. This may involve conducting a thorough investigation, requesting corrective actions or compensation from the vendor, or potentially terminating the contract and seeking alternative suppliers. Throughout the process, I would keep the employee and any affected customers or stakeholders informed of the progress and resolution of the complaint, and ensure that the company's response is timely, transparent, and focused on minimizing any negative impacts on the business. I would also use the situation as an opportunity to review and improve the company's vendor management and quality control processes, such as conducting more frequent audits, setting clearer performance metrics and penalties, and involving employees and customers in the feedback and selection of vendors. By taking a proactive and systematic approach to vendor quality and performance, the company can reduce the risk of disruptions, enhance its reputation and competitiveness, and create a culture of continuous improvement and customer focus.

91. Q: How would you handle a situation where an employee requests accommodation for a medical condition that requires frequent breaks and time off for appointments, but their colleagues are complaining about the perceived unfairness and the increased workload on the rest of the team?

A: I would approach this situation with a balance of empathy, fairness, and open communication. First, I would meet with the employee requesting the accommodation to discuss their needs and gather any necessary medical documentation, while assuring them of the confidentiality of their health information. I would then review the company's policies and legal obligations for providing reasonable accommodations under the Americans with Disabilities Act (ADA) and engage in an interactive process to determine if the requested accommodations are feasible and effective. If the accommodations are approved, I would work with the employee, their manager, and the rest of the team to develop a plan for implementing the accommodations in a way that minimizes disruption and resentment. This may involve redistributing work assignments, providing temporary or part-time support staff, or exploring flexible scheduling or remote work options that benefit the entire team. I would also provide education and training for the team on the importance and legal requirements of accommodating employees with disabilities, and foster a culture of empathy, inclusion, and mutual support. If the team's complaints persist or escalate, I would address them directly and remind them of the company's policies and values around non-discrimination, as well as the potential legal and reputational risks of creating a hostile or retaliatory environment for the employee with the disability. At the same time, I would acknowledge the team's concerns and work with them to find solutions that balance the needs and contributions of all team members, such as regular check-ins, recognition and rewards for extra efforts, or opportunities for skill development and advancement. Throughout the process, I would model and promote a spirit of collaboration, flexibility, and respect, and ensure that all employees feel heard, valued, and supported in bringing their whole selves to work.

92. Q: An employee's performance has been consistently poor, and they have been placed on a performance improvement plan. However, they are now claiming that the performance issues are due to a lack of clear goals and expectations from their manager, and they are requesting a transfer to a different department or manager. How would you handle this situation?

A: I would meet with the employee to discuss their concerns and gather more information about their perception of the goals and expectations for their role, as well as their reasons for requesting a transfer. I would then review the employee's job description, performance history, and improvement plan, as well as any documentation or feedback from their manager regarding the clarity and consistency of the goals and expectations. If there is evidence that the manager has not provided sufficient direction, support, or feedback to the employee, I would address this issue with the manager and provide coaching and resources to help them improve their performance management skills. I would also work with the employee and the manager to revise the improvement plan and set clear, measurable, and achievable goals and expectations for the employee's performance, along with regular check-ins and feedback sessions. If, after these interventions, the employee's performance still does not improve, I would consider their request for a transfer, but only if it is feasible and appropriate based on the available positions, the employee's skills and qualifications, and the potential impact on both departments. If a transfer is not possible or advisable, I would continue to hold the employee accountable to the revised improvement plan and take appropriate disciplinary action, up to and including termination, if they fail to meet the agreed-upon goals and expectations. Throughout the process, I would maintain objectivity, transparency, and consistency in applying the company's performance management policies and procedures, while also providing support and resources to help both the employee and the manager succeed in their roles.

93. Q: How would you handle a situation where an employee is consistently not meeting the company's standards for maintaining the confidentiality and security of customer data, such as leaving files or devices unattended, and their behavior is putting the company at risk of a data breach or legal liability?

A: I would treat this situation with the utmost seriousness and urgency, given the potential consequences of a data breach for the company's reputation, financial stability, and legal compliance. I would first review the company's policies, procedures, and training related to data privacy and security, as well as any relevant laws and regulations, such as HIPAA, GDPR, or state data protection laws. I would then meet with the employee to discuss the specific instances of their non-compliant behavior and the risks it poses to the company and its customers. I would provide them with a clear and detailed explanation of the policies and procedures they are violating, as well as the potential disciplinary actions and legal penalties for continued non-compliance. I would also work with the IT and security teams to conduct a thorough audit of the employee's access to and handling of customer data, and implement any necessary technical or administrative safeguards to prevent or detect further breaches. Depending on the severity and frequency of the employee's behavior, I may also involve legal counsel and senior management in the investigation and response. If the employee's behavior does not improve after the initial warning and remediation, I would follow the company's disciplinary procedures for data security violations, which may include suspension, termination, and referral to law enforcement. Throughout the process, I would maintain strict confidentiality and documentation of the investigation and any actions taken, and communicate with affected customers and stakeholders as required by law or company policy. I would also use the incident as an opportunity to review and strengthen the company's overall data security and privacy program, including regular training, auditing, and enforcement for all employees and third-party vendors.

94. Q: An employee submits a complaint about a colleague's behavior that is not illegal or a clear violation of company policy, but is making them feel

uncomfortable or disrespected, such as personal comments or jokes. How would you address this situation?

A: I would take the employee's complaint seriously and handle it with sensitivity and discretion, recognizing that behavior that is not illegal or a policy violation can still have a significant impact on an employee's well-being, productivity, and sense of belonging at work. I would meet with the employee who submitted the complaint to listen to their concerns, gather specific examples of the behavior, and understand the impact it is having on them. I would also assure them that retaliation for reporting concerns is strictly prohibited and that I will take appropriate steps to address the situation. I would then meet with the colleague who is the subject of the complaint to discuss the reported behavior and get their perspective, while maintaining the confidentiality of the complaining employee to the extent possible. I would provide the colleague with specific feedback on how their behavior is being perceived and the impact it is having, and clarify the company's expectations for respectful and professional conduct in the workplace. Depending on the nature and severity of the behavior, I may also recommend or require the colleague to participate in additional training, coaching, or counseling to help them develop greater self-awareness, empathy, and communication skills. If the behavior continues or escalates after this initial intervention, I would follow the company's progressive discipline process, which may include verbal warnings, written warnings, suspension, or termination, depending on the circumstances. Throughout the process, I would keep the complaining employee informed of the steps being taken and check in with them regularly to ensure that the situation has been resolved to their satisfaction and that they feel safe and supported at work. I would also use the incident as an opportunity to reinforce the company's values and expectations for a respectful and inclusive workplace culture, and provide resources and training for all employees on topics such as unconscious bias, microaggressions, and bystander intervention.

95. Q: How would you handle a situation where an employee requests an accommodation for a disability that would require significant changes to their job duties or the team's workflow, and their manager is resistant to the idea, citing concerns about productivity and fairness to other team members?

A: I would approach this situation with a commitment to finding a solution that meets both the employee's needs and the business's requirements, while complying with legal obligations and company policies. I would first meet with the employee to discuss their specific accommodation request, gather any necessary medical documentation, and understand how the requested changes would enable them to perform the essential functions of their job. I would then meet with the manager to discuss their concerns and explore the potential impact of the accommodation on the team's workflow, productivity, and morale. I would provide the manager with information and training on the company's legal obligations under the ADA and the benefits of creating an inclusive and accommodating workplace for all employees. I would also work with the manager and the HR team to conduct an analysis of the employee's job duties and identify any essential functions that cannot be modified or eliminated without causing undue hardship to the business. Based on this analysis, I would work with the employee, the manager, and any other relevant stakeholders to develop an accommodation plan that balances the employee's needs with the team's operational requirements. This may involve job restructuring, reassignment of marginal duties, the use of assistive technology or equipment, or flexible scheduling arrangements. If the manager continues to resist the accommodation plan, I would escalate the issue to higher levels of management and/or legal counsel to ensure compliance with the ADA and prevent any potential discrimination or retaliation against the employee. Throughout the process, I would maintain open and respectful communication with all parties, document all discussions and decisions, and seek to create a culture of inclusion and support for employees with disabilities. I would also use the situation as an opportunity to review and improve the company's overall accommodation process and provide training and resources for managers on how to effectively manage and support diverse teams.

96. Q: An employee's performance has been consistently excellent, but they are now exhibiting signs of stress and burnout, and have confided in you that they are considering leaving the company for a less demanding job. How would you handle this situation?

A: I would approach this situation with empathy, concern, and a focus on retaining a valuable employee while supporting their well-being and career goals. I would start by meeting with the employee to express my appreciation for their contributions and performance, and create a safe and confidential space for them to share more about the factors contributing to their stress and burnout. I would listen actively and non-judgmentally to their concerns, and explore the specific aspects of their job or work environment that are causing them distress, such as workload, lack of support or resources, or conflicts with colleagues or managers. Based on this conversation, I would work with the employee to develop a plan for addressing their stressors and improving their job satisfaction and well-being. This may involve adjustments to their workload or responsibilities, additional support or resources, professional development opportunities, or changes to their work schedule or environment. I would also provide the employee with information and referrals to relevant company benefits and programs, such as the Employee Assistance Program (EAP), wellness initiatives, or stress management training. If the employee expresses a desire to explore other career opportunities, either within or outside the company, I would support them in that process and provide guidance and resources for job searching, resume writing, and interviewing skills. At the same time, I would work with the employee's manager and other relevant stakeholders to develop a retention plan that addresses the employee's concerns and demonstrates the company's commitment to their growth and development. This may involve creating a career development plan, providing additional recognition or compensation, or offering new challenges or leadership opportunities that align with the employee's strengths and interests. Throughout the process, I would maintain open and supportive communication with the employee, while also setting clear expectations and boundaries around job performance and professional conduct. I would also use the situation as an opportunity to review and improve the company's overall approach to employee well-being, engagement, and retention, and provide training and resources for managers on how to recognize and prevent burnout and support the mental health and career development of their team members.

97. Q: How would you handle a situation where an employee is consistently not meeting the company's standards for maintaining a respectful and inclusive work environment, such as making derogatory comments or jokes about certain groups, and their behavior is causing other employees to feel uncomfortable or discriminated against?

A: I would treat this situation with the utmost seriousness and urgency, recognizing that discriminatory or harassing behavior not only violates company policy and legal standards but also undermines the psychological safety, diversity, and productivity of the entire organization. I would first gather information about the specific instances of the employee's behavior, including any complaints, witnesses, or documentation, and review the company's policies and training related to harassment, discrimination, and respectful workplace conduct. I would then meet with the employee to discuss the reported behavior and its impact on their colleagues and the work environment. I would provide them with specific examples of the offensive comments or jokes, and explain how they violate company policy and create a hostile or discriminatory atmosphere for other employees. I would also make it clear that such behavior is unacceptable and will not be tolerated, and outline the potential disciplinary consequences, up to and including termination, for continued violations. Depending on the severity and frequency of the behavior, I may also require the employee to participate in additional training, counseling, or remedial action to address the underlying attitudes or biases that are contributing to their behavior. I would also meet with the employees who have been impacted by the behavior to express support and empathy, offer resources such as the EAP or a designated diversity and inclusion representative, and assure them that appropriate action is being taken to address the situation and prevent future incidents.

Throughout the process, I would maintain strict confidentiality and documentation, following the company's procedures for investigating and resolving harassment and discrimination complaints. I would also communicate with senior management and legal counsel as needed to ensure compliance with all relevant laws and regulations, and to coordinate any necessary public relations or crisis management response. Finally, I would use the incident as an opportunity to reinforce the company's commitment to diversity, equity, and inclusion, and provide training and resources for all employees on topics such as unconscious bias, cultural competence, and allyship. By taking a strong and proactive stance against discriminatory behavior and creating a culture of respect and belonging, the company can not only prevent future incidents but also attract and retain a more diverse and engaged workforce.

98. Q: An employee submits a complaint about a customer's behavior that is not illegal but is making them feel uncomfortable or disrespected, such as flirtatious comments or personal questions. How would you address this situation?

    A: I would take the employee's complaint seriously and handle it with sensitivity and professionalism, recognizing that customer behavior that is not illegal can still have a significant impact on an employee's well-being, productivity, and sense of safety at work. I would meet with the employee who submitted the complaint to listen to their concerns, gather specific examples of the behavior, and understand the impact it is having on them. I would also assure them that the company takes their comfort and well-being seriously and that I will take appropriate steps to address the situation. I would then review the company's policies and procedures related to customer service, harassment, and workplace safety, as well as any relevant laws or regulations. Depending on the nature and severity of the behavior, I may also consult with legal counsel or senior management to determine the appropriate course of action. If the behavior is relatively minor or isolated, I may start by coaching the employee on how to set boundaries and communicate assertively with the customer, while also providing them with additional support or resources, such as a buddy system or a script for handling difficult interactions. If the behavior is more severe or persistent, I may need to intervene directly with the customer, either by speaking with them myself or escalating the issue to their supervisor or company. I would explain the specific behavior that is causing concern and the impact it is having on our employee, and request that they cease the behavior immediately and treat our employee with respect and professionalism. If the customer is unwilling or unable to comply with this request, I may need to take further action, such as reassigning the employee to a different account or terminating the business relationship altogether. Throughout the process, I would keep the employee informed of the steps being taken and check in with them regularly to ensure that the situation has been resolved to their satisfaction and that they feel safe and supported at work. I would also document all interactions and decisions related to the complaint, in case further action is needed. Finally, I would use the incident as an opportunity to review and improve the company's overall approach to customer service and workplace safety, and provide training and resources for all employees on how to handle difficult or inappropriate customer behavior while maintaining their own well-being and professionalism.

99. Q: How would you handle a situation where an employee requests accommodation for a medical condition that would require them to work from home permanently, but their job duties involve regular in-person interactions with colleagues and customers?

A: I would approach this situation with a goal of finding a reasonable accommodation that balances the employee's medical needs with the essential functions and requirements of their job, while also complying with legal obligations and company policies. I would start by meeting with the employee to discuss their specific accommodation request, gather any necessary medical documentation, and understand how working from home would enable them to perform their job duties safely and effectively. I would also explain the company's process for determining reasonable accommodations and the factors that will be considered, such as the essential functions of the job, the impact on business operations, and the feasibility of alternative accommodations. I would then meet with the employee's manager and other relevant stakeholders to review the employee's job description and analyze the essential functions and requirements of the role. This may involve identifying which duties can be performed remotely, which require in-person interaction, and which can be modified or reassigned without causing undue hardship to the business. Based on this analysis, I would explore alternative accommodations that may meet the employee's needs while also allowing them to perform the essential functions of their job, such as a hybrid remote/in-person schedule, the use of virtual communication tools, or the reassignment of certain duties to other team members. If an alternative accommodation is not feasible or effective, I would consider whether the employee can be reassigned to a different role that can be performed entirely remotely, or whether a leave of absence or other arrangement may be necessary until the employee's medical condition improves or changes. Throughout the process, I would maintain open and respectful communication with the employee and their medical providers, document all discussions and decisions, and seek guidance from legal counsel and senior management as needed to ensure compliance with the ADA and other relevant laws and regulations. I would also provide support and resources for the employee's manager and team to help them adjust to any changes in workflow or communication resulting from the accommodation. Ultimately, my goal would be to find a solution that allows the employee to continue contributing their skills and experience to the company while also prioritizing their health and well-being.

100. Q: An employee's performance has been consistently poor, and they have been placed on a performance improvement plan. However, they are now claiming that the performance issues are due to a personality clash with their manager, and they are threatening to file a harassment complaint if they are not transferred to a different team or given a new manager. How would you handle this situation?

A: I would approach this situation with a commitment to investigating the employee's claims thoroughly and objectively, while also holding them accountable for their performance and behavior. I would start by meeting with the employee to listen to their concerns and gather specific examples of the alleged harassment or personality clash with their manager. I would explain the company's process for investigating harassment complaints and the potential consequences for making false or retaliatory claims. I would also review the employee's performance history and improvement plan, and clarify the specific expectations and metrics they are required to meet in order to demonstrate satisfactory performance. I would then meet with the employee's manager to discuss the employee's allegations and get their perspective on the situation. I would ask the manager to provide specific examples of the employee's performance issues and the steps they have taken to address them, as well as any documentation or feedback they have provided to the employee. I would also explore whether there have been any communication breakdowns, misunderstandings, or interpersonal conflicts between the manager and employee that may be contributing to the performance issues. Based on these initial conversations, I would determine whether there is sufficient evidence to warrant a formal investigation into the harassment complaint, or whether the performance issues are unrelated to any alleged harassment or personality clash. If an investigation is necessary, I would follow the company's procedures for conducting a prompt, thorough, and impartial inquiry, which may involve interviewing witnesses, reviewing documentation, and consulting with legal counsel. If the investigation reveals that the manager has engaged in harassment or discrimination, I would take appropriate disciplinary action, up to and including termination, and work with the employee to determine an appropriate resolution, such as a transfer to a different team or a change in reporting structure. However, if the investigation does not substantiate the harassment complaint, or if the performance issues are found to be unrelated to any alleged harassment, I would communicate this to the employee and continue to hold them accountable to the performance improvement plan. I would also work with the manager to provide additional coaching, feedback, and support to help the employee meet the required standards, while also setting clear expectations around professional conduct and communication. If the employee's performance does not improve after a reasonable period of time, I would proceed with the appropriate disciplinary action, up to and including termination, based on the company's policies and the terms of the improvement plan. Throughout the process, I would maintain strict confidentiality and documentation, and ensure that all parties are treated with respect and fairness, regardless of the outcome of the complaint or the performance issues. I would also use the situation as an opportunity to review and improve the company's overall approach to performance management, employee relations, and harassment prevention, and provide training and resources for managers and employees on how to create a positive and productive work environment.

101. Q: How would you handle a situation where an employee is consistently not meeting the company's standards for maintaining a safe and hygienic work environment, such as not following proper cleaning protocols or not wearing required personal protective equipment (PPE)?

A: I would approach this situation with a focus on education, accountability, and the health and safety of all employees. I would start by meeting with the employee to discuss the specific instances of non-compliance and the potential risks and consequences of their behavior. I would provide them with a clear and detailed explanation of the company's safety and hygiene policies, as well as any relevant laws or regulations, such as OSHA standards. I would also ensure that they have received the necessary training and have access to the required PPE and cleaning supplies. If the employee's behavior is due to a lack of understanding or resources, I would work with their manager to provide additional training, coaching, and support to help them meet the required standards. However, if the employee's behavior is willful or negligent, I would follow the company's disciplinary procedures for safety violations, which may include verbal warnings, written warnings, suspension, or termination, depending on the severity and frequency of the violations. I would also work with the facilities and operations teams to conduct regular audits and inspections to ensure compliance with safety and hygiene protocols, and to identify and address any systemic issues or hazards. Throughout the process, I would emphasize the importance of maintaining a safe and healthy work environment for all employees, and the shared responsibility of each individual to follow the established policies and procedures. I would also use the situation as an opportunity to review and improve the company's overall approach to safety and hygiene training, communication, and enforcement, and to foster a culture of continuous improvement and accountability.

102. Q: An employee submits a complaint about a vendor's unethical business practices, such as using child labor or engaging in environmental damage, but the vendor is a key supplier for the company's products and has a long-standing relationship with senior management. How would you address this situation?

A: I would take the employee's complaint seriously and handle it with the utmost professionalism, integrity, and transparency, recognizing that the company's reputation and values are at stake. I would start by meeting with the employee to gather more information about the specific allegations and any evidence or sources they have to support their claims. I would also explain the company's process for investigating and addressing ethical complaints, and assure them that there will be no retaliation for raising concerns in good faith. I would then review the vendor's contract, code of conduct, and any relevant industry standards or regulations to determine if the alleged practices violate any legal or ethical obligations. I would also consult with the company's legal, compliance, and corporate social responsibility teams to assess the potential risks and impacts of the situation. Based on this initial assessment, I would escalate the complaint to the appropriate level of management and recommend a course of action, which may include conducting a thorough investigation, engaging an independent auditor, or suspending or terminating the business relationship with the vendor, depending on the severity and credibility of the allegations. I would also work with the procurement and supply chain teams to identify and vet alternative suppliers that align with the company's ethical standards and business needs. Throughout the process, I would keep the employee and other relevant stakeholders informed of the progress and outcomes of the investigation, while also maintaining confidentiality and protecting the vendor's due process rights. I would also ensure that the company's response is consistent with its stated values and policies, and that any decisions are based on objective and verifiable facts rather than personal relationships or business pressures. Finally, I would use the situation as an opportunity to review and strengthen the company's overall approach to ethical sourcing, supplier management, and employee reporting, and to provide training and resources for all employees on how to identify and report unethical conduct in the workplace and the supply chain.

103. Q: How would you handle a situation where an employee requests accommodation for a disability that would require the company to purchase expensive equipment or software, but the budget for accommodations is limited and there are other pending requests from other employees?

A: I would approach this situation with a commitment to finding a fair and effective solution that balances the employee's needs, the company's resources, and the legal requirements for providing reasonable accommodations. I would start by meeting with the employee to discuss their specific accommodation request, gather any necessary medical documentation, and understand how the requested equipment or software would enable them to perform the essential functions of their job. I would also explain the company's process for evaluating and prioritizing accommodation requests, and the factors that will be considered, such as the nature and severity of the disability, the effectiveness of the accommodation, and the cost and feasibility of implementation.

I would then review the company's budget and policies for accommodations, as well as any relevant laws or regulations, such as the ADA or state disability laws. I would also consult with the IT, procurement, and finance teams to determine the specific costs and technical requirements of the requested equipment or software, and to explore alternative solutions that may be more cost-effective or efficient.

Based on this analysis, I would work with the employee and their manager to develop an accommodation plan that meets the employee's needs while also considering the company's resources and other pending requests. This may involve identifying alternative equipment or software that provides similar functionality at a lower cost, or exploring other accommodations that may be effective, such as remote work, flexible scheduling, or job restructuring.

If the requested accommodation is determined to be reasonable and necessary, but the cost exceeds the available budget, I would work with senior management to explore options for securing additional funding or reallocating resources from other areas of the business. I would also consider whether the accommodation could be phased in over time or shared among multiple employees with similar needs.

If, after exploring all options, the requested accommodation is determined to be an undue hardship for the company, I would communicate this decision to the employee in a clear, respectful, and well-documented manner, and work with them to identify alternative accommodations or resources that may be available, such as government or community-based programs for assistive technology.

Throughout the process, I would maintain open and transparent communication with the employee and all relevant stakeholders, and ensure that all accommodation decisions are based on objective and consistent criteria, rather than personal biases or assumptions. I would also use the situation as an opportunity to review and improve the company's overall approach to disability inclusion and accommodation, and to provide training and resources for managers and employees on how to create a welcoming and accessible workplace for all.

104. Q: An employee's performance has been consistently poor, and they have been placed on a performance improvement plan. However, they are now claiming that the performance issues are due to a personal crisis, such as a family illness or financial hardship, and they are requesting more time and flexibility to improve. How would you handle this situation?

A: I would approach this situation with empathy, compassion, and a focus on finding a solution that supports the employee's well-being while also holding them accountable for their performance. I would start by meeting with the employee to listen to their concerns and gather more information about the specific personal crisis they are facing, and how it is impacting their work. I would express my support and understanding, and assure them that the company values their contributions and wants to help them succeed.

I would then review the employee's performance history and improvement plan, as well as any relevant company policies or benefits related to personal leave, employee assistance, or accommodations. Based on this information, I would work with the employee and their manager to develop a revised performance improvement plan that takes into account their personal circumstances and provides reasonable accommodations or flexibility, such as a temporary reduction in workload, additional time off, or access to counseling or financial planning services.

However, I would also make it clear that the revised plan is not a waiver of the company's performance expectations, and that the employee is still responsible for meeting the agreed-upon goals and metrics within a reasonable timeframe. I would set clear expectations for communication, accountability, and progress monitoring, and provide regular feedback and support to help the employee stay on track.

If, after a reasonable period of time and despite the accommodations and support provided, the employee's performance does not improve to a satisfactory level, I would proceed with the appropriate disciplinary action, up to and including termination, based on the company's policies and the terms of the improvement plan. However, I would do so with compassion and respect, and ensure that the employee is treated fairly and given due process throughout the process.

I would also use the situation as an opportunity to review and improve the company's overall approach to employee well-being, crisis management, and performance management, and to provide training and resources for managers on how to support and engage employees who may be facing personal or professional challenges. By creating a culture of empathy, flexibility, and accountability, the company can help all employees to thrive and contribute their best work, even in difficult times.

105. Q: How would you handle a situation where an employee is consistently not meeting the company's standards for maintaining confidentiality of sensitive information, such as discussing client details or business strategies with outside parties, and their behavior is putting the company at risk of legal or competitive harm?

A: I would approach this situation with the utmost seriousness and urgency, recognizing that breaches of confidentiality can have severe consequences for the company's reputation, legal liability, and competitive advantage.I would start by gathering all available information and evidence related to the employee's behavior, including any specific incidents, witnesses, or documentation. I would also review the company's policies, procedures, and training related to confidentiality and data protection, as well as any relevant laws, regulations, or contractual obligations.

I would then meet with the employee to discuss the reported behavior and the potential consequences of their actions. I would provide specific examples of the breaches of confidentiality and explain how they violate company policy and put the business at risk. I would also give the employee an opportunity to respond and provide any explanations or mitigating factors.

Depending on the severity and frequency of the breaches, I would take appropriate disciplinary action, which may include verbal warnings, written warnings, suspension, or termination of employment. I would also work with the legal and IT departments to assess the extent of the damage and take steps to contain and remediate any unauthorized disclosures, such as notifying affected clients or partners, revoking access privileges, or implementing additional security measures.

In parallel, I would work with the employee's manager and the HR team to investigate the root causes of the behavior and identify any systemic issues or gaps in training, communication, or oversight that may have contributed to the problem. Based on this analysis, I would develop and implement a plan to strengthen the company's overall approach to confidentiality and data protection, which may include:
- Updating and clarifying policies and procedures related to confidentiality, including acceptable use of technology, social media, and external communications

- Providing mandatory training and regular reminders for all employees on the importance of confidentiality and the consequences of breaches

- Implementing technical controls and monitoring systems to prevent and detect unauthorized access or disclosure of sensitive information

- Establishing clear roles, responsibilities, and accountability for managing and protecting confidential data across the organization

- Conducting regular audits and risk assessments to identify and address potential vulnerabilities or areas for improvement

Throughout the process, I would maintain clear, consistent, and well-documented communication with all relevant stakeholders, including the employee, their manager, senior leadership, and any affected clients or partners. I would also ensure that the company's response is proportionate, fair, and compliant with all applicable laws and regulations.

Finally, I would use the incident as a teachable moment to reinforce the company's values and expectations around integrity, trust, and professionalism, and to foster a culture of vigilance, responsibility, and continuous improvement in protecting the company's most valuable assets.

106. Q: An employee submits a complaint about a customer's inappropriate behavior, such as making racist or sexist comments, but the customer is a high-value client and the employee is concerned about losing their business. How would you address this situation?

A: I would approach this situation with a clear and unwavering commitment to creating a safe, respectful, and inclusive environment for all employees, regardless of the status or value of any customer or client.

I would start by meeting with the employee who submitted the complaint to listen to their concerns, gather specific details about the incidents, and express my support and appreciation for their willingness to speak up. I would assure them that the company takes all reports of harassment or discrimination seriously and will take appropriate action to address the situation.

I would then review the company's policies and procedures related to customer conduct, harassment, and non-discrimination, as well as any relevant laws or regulations. I would also consult with the legal department and senior leadership to assess the potential risks and impacts of the situation, both for the employee and for the business.

Based on this assessment, I would develop a plan of action to address the customer's behavior and protect the employee from further harm. This may include:

- Directly addressing the behavior with the customer, either through a phone call, email, or in-person meeting, and clearly communicating the company's expectations for respectful and professional conduct

- Assigning a different representative or account manager to handle the customer's business, to minimize the employee's exposure to the harassing behavior

- Offering the employee additional support, such as counseling, time off, or reassignment to a different role or client

- Documenting all incidents and interactions related to the complaint, in case further action is needed, such as terminating the business relationship or pursuing legal remedies

The priority in this situation would be to ensure the safety and well-being of the employee, while also taking appropriate steps to address the customer's unacceptable behavior. Even if the customer is a high-value client, the company's commitment to maintaining a respectful and inclusive workplace must take precedence.

107. Q: An employee comes to you with concerns about a manager who is consistently late to meetings, frequently leaves early, and is generally disengaged. However, this manager is highly skilled and delivers excellent results. How would you handle this situation?

A: I would first have a private conversation with the employee to fully understand their concerns and gather specific details about the manager's behavior. I would express appreciation for them bringing this issue to my attention and assure them that I will look into it.
Next, I would meet with the manager to address the concerns in a constructive manner. I would start by acknowledging their strong performance and contributions, but then tactfully discuss the reports of their unprofessional conduct. I would emphasize the importance of setting a good example and maintaining high standards of accountability, regardless of one's technical skills or results.

Depending on the manager's response, I may recommend additional training or coaching to help them improve their time management and leadership skills. I would also implement a performance improvement plan with clear expectations and deadlines. If the behavior persists, I would not hesitate to take disciplinary action, up to and including termination, as the company's policies and values must be upheld consistently.

My goal would be to address the performance issues head-on, while also providing the manager with the support and resources they need to improve. Maintaining a high-performing, engaged, and accountable leadership team is critical, and I would not compromise those standards even for a top performer.

108. Q: You receive an anonymous report that a manager is bullying and verbally abusing their team. The manager is a long-term, high-performing employee who brings in a significant amount of revenue. How would you investigate and address this situation?

A: I would take this anonymous report very seriously, as any allegations of bullying or verbal abuse must be investigated thoroughly, regardless of the employee's tenure or performance record.

First, I would review the company's policies on harassment, discrimination, and workplace conduct. I would then develop a plan to gather more information and conduct a fair and impartial investigation. This would likely involve:

- Interviewing the anonymous reporter (if possible) to get more details

- Interviewing other team members to corroborate the claims or identify any patterns of behavior

- Reviewing any documentation, such as emails, Slack messages, or performance reviews, that could provide evidence

- Meeting with the accused manager to hear their side of the story and give them an opportunity to respond

Throughout the investigation, I would maintain strict confidentiality to protect the anonymity of the reporter and ensure the process is fair for all involved.

If the allegations are substantiated, I would take immediate action to address the manager's behavior. This could include:

- Providing the manager with formal coaching and training on appropriate leadership skills and conflict resolution

- Implementing a performance improvement plan with clear expectations and consequences

- Suspending or demoting the manager if the behavior is severe enough

- Terminating the manager's employment if the behavior is egregious and cannot be remedied

The company's commitment to a respectful, inclusive, and professional workplace must take precedence, even for high-performing employees. I would not hesitate to take the necessary steps to uphold those values and protect the wellbeing of the team.

109. Q: An employee comes to you and expresses concerns about a coworker who is frequently late, takes extended breaks, and leaves early, but still manages to meet their deadlines. The employee feels this is unfair and wants you to address it. How would you handle this situation?

A: I would first have a private conversation with the employee to fully understand their concerns and get more details about the coworker's behavior. I would validate their feelings of unfairness and assure them that I will look into the situation.

Next, I would review the company's policies and procedures around attendance, work hours, and performance management. I would also check if there are any extenuating circumstances or accommodations that may be impacting the coworker's schedule.

I would then meet with the coworker to discuss the concerns that have been raised. I would approach the conversation in a constructive manner, focusing on the impact of their behavior on the team and the company's expectations for professionalism and accountability.

During this meeting, I would gather the coworker's perspective and see if there are any legitimate reasons for their attendance or scheduling issues. If so, I would work with them to find a reasonable solution, such as adjusting their hours or providing additional support.

However, if the coworker's behavior is simply a matter of poor time management or disregard for the company's policies, I would outline clear performance expectations and consequences for continued non-compliance. This could include:

- Verbal warning to immediately address the attendance issues

- Written warning outlining a performance improvement plan with specific goals and deadlines

- Suspension or demotion if the behavior does not improve

- Termination if the issues persist and the coworker remains unwilling to change

Throughout the process, I would continue to communicate openly with the concerned employee. I would assure them that their concerns are being taken seriously and that I am committed to ensuring fairness and consistency across the team.

However, I would also emphasize that personnel decisions must be based on objective performance criteria, not personal feelings of unfairness. My role is to uphold the company's policies and ensure all employees are held to the same standards, regardless of their individual work styles or results.

The key is to balance the legitimate concerns of the reporting employee with the need to address performance issues in a fair and transparent manner. By taking a measured, policy-driven approach, I can demonstrate the company's commitment to creating an equitable workplace while also holding all employees accountable.

110. Q: An employee comes to you and expresses concerns that their manager is playing favorites and unfairly distributing work assignments and development opportunities. The employee feels this is negatively impacting their career growth. How would you handle this situation?

A: I would take these concerns very seriously, as allegations of favoritism and unfair treatment can have a significant impact on employee morale, engagement, and retention.

First, I would have a private conversation with the employee to fully understand the specifics of their concerns. I would ask for concrete examples of how the manager is distributing work and development opportunities, and how the employee feels this is unfairly impacting them.

Next, I would review the company's policies and procedures around performance management, career development, and employee complaints. I would also check if there are any documented performance reviews, feedback, or other records that could shed light on the situation.

I would then meet with the manager to discuss the employee's concerns. I would approach this conversation in a collaborative manner, aiming to understand the manager's perspective and decision-making process. However, I would also make it clear that any evidence of favoritism or unfair treatment is unacceptable and must be addressed.

Depending on the findings of my investigation, I may take the following actions:

- Provide the manager with coaching and training on effective, equitable management practices

- Implement a more structured, transparent system for work assignments and development opportunities

- Conduct a comprehensive review of the team's performance and development plans to ensure fairness

- Transfer the employee to a different team or manager if the issues cannot be resolved

- Issue disciplinary action against the manager if the favoritism is severe or repeated

Throughout this process, I would continue to communicate openly with the employee, providing updates on the steps being taken and reassuring them that their concerns are being taken seriously. My goal would be to restore a sense of fairness and trust within the team, while also upholding the company's commitment to meritocracy and equal opportunity.

111. Q: You receive an anonymous report that a manager is misusing company funds for personal expenses. The manager is a long-time, high-performing

employee who is well-liked by leadership. How would you investigate and address this situation?

A: I would take this situation very seriously, as the misuse of company funds is a significant breach of trust and fiduciary responsibility, regardless of the manager's tenure or performance record.

First, I would gather as much information as possible to understand the scope and nature of the misuse of funds. This would likely involve:

- Reviewing the manager's expense reports, credit card statements, and other financial records

- Interviewing the manager to get their side of the story and understand their rationale

- Consulting with the finance and accounting teams to identify any discrepancies or red flags

- Determining if there are any company policies or legal regulations that have been violated

Once I have a clear picture of what has occurred, I would meet with the manager to confront them with the evidence and give them an opportunity to respond. Depending on their reaction and the severity of the offense, I may suspend them from their duties pending further investigation.

I would then consult with the company's legal counsel to understand the appropriate disciplinary actions and potential legal consequences. This could include:

- Requiring the manager to repay the misused funds
- Issuing a final written warning with clear performance expectations
- Demotion or reassignment to a non-financial role
- Termination of employment

Regardless of the outcome, I would document the entire investigation process and ensure that any disciplinary actions are consistent with the company's policies and procedures. I would also consider whether any systemic changes are needed to improve financial controls and oversight.

Throughout this process, I would be mindful of maintaining confidentiality and treating the manager with professionalism, even if the allegations are substantiated. My goal would be to address the misconduct firmly while also preserving the integrity of the investigation and the company's reputation.

112. Q: How would you handle a situation where an employee is consistently not meeting the company's standards for maintaining confidentiality of customer information, and their behavior is putting the company at risk of a data breach?

A: I would first review the company's policies and procedures for data privacy and security, as well as the specific instances of the employee's behavior and the potential consequences of a data breach. I would then meet with the employee to discuss the severity of the issue and the importance of maintaining the confidentiality of customer information. I would provide additional training and resources on data privacy best practices and the company's security protocols, and work with the IT department to implement additional technical safeguards and monitoring of the employee's access to sensitive data. If the employee's behavior does not improve despite these interventions, I would follow the company's disciplinary procedures for data privacy violations, which may include suspension, termination, and legal action depending on the severity and frequency of the violations. I would also work with the legal and PR departments to develop a response plan for any potential data breaches or customer complaints related to the employee's behavior. Throughout the process, I would emphasize the critical importance of data privacy and security for the trust and loyalty of our customers, and the serious consequences of any breaches or violations.

113. Q: An employee comes to you to report that their manager has been making inappropriate comments and unwanted physical contact, such as hugs or shoulder massages. The employee is concerned about retaliation if they file a formal complaint. How would you handle this situation?

A: As the HR Manager, I would take this report of inappropriate comments and physical contact by the manager extremely seriously. The employee's concerns about potential retaliation are also valid and understandable. First, I would assure the employee that their complaint will be investigated thoroughly and confidentially, and that the company has a strict non-retaliation policy that protects employees who report misconduct. I would encourage the employee to document any specific incidents they have experienced, including dates, times, witnesses (if any), and details of the inappropriate behavior. Next, I would schedule a private meeting with the accused manager to discuss the allegations, explain that a complaint has been made and an investigation will be opened, and advise the manager that any retaliatory actions would be grounds for disciplinary action. During the investigation, I would interview any relevant witnesses and review available documentation or security footage, maintaining strict confidentiality throughout the process. If the allegations are substantiated, I would recommend appropriate disciplinary action against the manager, and work with the reporting employee to ensure they feel safe and supported in the workplace going forward. Regardless of the outcome, I would document the entire investigation process thoroughly and review the company's harassment and discrimination policies to identify any areas that may need to be strengthened.

> 114. Q: How would you handle a situation where an employee is consistently late to work, despite multiple conversations and warnings?

A: I would first review the company's attendance and punctuality policies to understand the specific guidelines and disciplinary procedures in place. I would then schedule a private meeting with the employee to discuss the issue. During the meeting, I would:

- Clearly explain the importance of punctuality and the impact the employee's tardiness is having on their work and the team.

- Review the previous warnings and conversations about the issue, and ensure the employee understands the consequences of continued tardiness.

- Work with the employee to understand the reasons behind their lateness and see if there are any accommodations or solutions we can implement to help them improve their punctuality.

- Set clear expectations and a timeline for improvement, with specific consequences if the behavior does not change.

- Document the meeting and any agreed-upon action plan.

If the employee's behavior does not improve within the specified timeline, I would follow the company's progressive disciplinary process, which may include written warnings, suspension, and ultimately termination if the tardiness persists. Throughout the process, I would maintain open communication with the employee, provide support where possible, and ensure consistency in applying the company's policies.

> 115. Q: An employee approaches you about a conflict they are having with a coworker. They feel the coworker is undermining their work and making rude comments. How would you handle this situation?

A: I would first meet privately with the employee to fully understand the nature of the conflict and get specific details about the coworker's behavior. I would assure the employee that I will investigate the issue thoroughly and maintain confidentiality throughout the process.

Next, I would first meet privately with the employee to fully understand the nature of the conflict and get specific details about the coworker's behavior. I would assure the employee that I will investigate the issue thoroughly and maintain confidentiality throughout the process.

Next, I would schedule a meeting with the coworker to discuss the employee's concerns. I would approach the conversation in a calm and non-confrontational manner, explaining that I have received a complaint about their behavior and that it is impacting the work environment. I would give the coworker an opportunity to provide their perspective and understand their side of the story.

During the meeting, I would reiterate the company's policies regarding respectful workplace conduct and prohibitions on harassment or undermining behavior. I would make it clear that the behavior needs to stop immediately and that continued issues could result in disciplinary action.

I would then follow up with both employees separately to ensure the situation has been resolved and there is no further conflict or retaliation. I would document all discussions and actions taken, and continue to monitor the situation closely.

If the issues persist despite the initial intervention, I would consider more formal disciplinary measures, such as written warnings or temporary reassignment, to address the problematic behavior and restore a productive working relationship between the two employees. My goal would be to find a fair and constructive resolution that maintains a healthy work environment for all.

116. Q: An employee requests a significant raise, citing increased responsibilities and performance. However, the company's budget does not currently allow for large salary increases. How would you handle this conversation?

A: I would schedule a private meeting with the employee to discuss their request. I would acknowledge their contributions and the additional responsibilities they have taken on. However, I would also explain the company's current budgetary constraints and salary increase guidelines. I would propose alternative ways to recognize their performance, such as a smaller raise, a one-time bonus, additional benefits, or opportunities for professional development. I would emphasize that their contributions are valued, and work with them to find a mutually agreeable solution that aligns with the company's compensation policies. Throughout the discussion, I would maintain an open and empathetic tone, and explore creative ways to address the employee's needs within the company's financial limitations.

117. Q: You discover that an employee has been using company resources, such as computers and printers, for personal business activities during work hours. How would you address this issue?

A: I would first review the company's policies regarding the use of company equipment and resources. I would then schedule a private meeting with the employee to discuss the situation. During the meeting, I would:

- Clearly explain the policy violation and the reasons why it is unacceptable, such as lost productivity, potential security risks, and unfair use of company assets.

- Provide the employee an opportunity to explain their actions and understand their perspective.

- Emphasize the importance of using company resources solely for business purposes and the potential disciplinary consequences of continued misuse.

- Warn the employee that further violations may result in progressive disciplinary action, up to and including termination.

- Document the meeting and any agreed-upon corrective actions.

If the employee's behavior does not improve after the initial discussion, I would follow the company's disciplinary procedures, which may include written warnings, suspension, or termination, depending on the severity and frequency of the violations.

118. Q: An employee approaches you with concerns about their manager's management style, stating that the manager is often condescending, micromanages their work, and does not provide clear direction. How would you address this situation?

A: I would first assure the employee that their concerns will be taken seriously and investigated thoroughly. I would encourage the employee to provide specific examples of the manager's behavior and its impact on their work and the team.

Next, I would schedule a private meeting with the manager to discuss the employee's feedback. I would approach the conversation in a constructive manner, avoiding accusatory language and instead focusing on the need to improve the manager-employee relationship and work environment. I would ask the manager for their perspective on the situation and work collaboratively to identify ways they can adjust their management style to be more effective and supportive.

Potential solutions could include providing the manager with additional training or coaching on effective leadership and communication skills, setting clear performance expectations, and implementing regular check-ins and feedback mechanisms between the manager and their direct reports.

If the manager is unwilling or unable to make the necessary changes, I would consider reassigning the employee to a different team or manager, or, as a last resort, recommend disciplinary action against the manager, up to and including termination, if the behavior persists and negatively impacts the team's productivity and morale.

Throughout the process, I would maintain confidentiality, document all discussions and actions taken, and follow up with the employee to ensure their concerns have been addressed and the work environment has improved.

119. Q: You receive an anonymous complaint alleging that a manager is engaging in favoritism and unfair treatment of certain employees. How would you investigate and address this issue?

A: I would take this anonymous complaint very seriously, as allegations of favoritism and unfair treatment can significantly undermine morale, trust, and the overall work environment. I would first review the company's policies and procedures related to performance management, promotions, and disciplinary actions to understand the guidelines and expectations around fair and equitable treatment of employees.
Next, I would launch a thorough and impartial investigation, while maintaining the confidentiality of the complainant. This would involve:

- Reviewing the performance records, disciplinary actions, and promotion histories of the employees under the accused manager's supervision to identify any patterns or discrepancies.

- Conducting confidential interviews with a sample of the manager's direct reports, as well as the manager themselves, to gather more information about the alleged favoritism and unfair treatment.

- Analyzing any available documentation, such as meeting notes, emails, or performance reviews, that could provide further insight into the manager's decision-making and treatment of employees.

If the investigation substantiates the allegations of favoritism and unfair treatment, I would take immediate corrective action. This could include:

- Providing the manager with additional training and coaching on equitable management practices.

- Implementing stricter oversight and accountability measures for the manager's decision-making processes.

- Considering disciplinary action against the manager, up to and including termination, if the behavior is severe or persistent.

- Reviewing and potentially adjusting any affected employment decisions, such as promotions or disciplinary actions, to ensure fairness.

- Communicating the findings and corrective actions to the employees involved, while maintaining confidentiality.

Throughout the process, I would document all steps taken and ensure that the company's policies and procedures are being consistently applied. The goal would be to address the issue, restore trust and fairness in the workplace, and implement measures to prevent similar problems from occurring in the future.

120. Q: An employee informs you that they are experiencing a personal crisis, such as a family emergency or medical issue, and needs to take an extended leave of absence. How would you handle this request?

A: I would first express empathy and understanding for the employee's situation. I would then review the company's policies and procedures regarding leave of absence, including any applicable federal or state laws such as the Family and Medical Leave Act

(FMLA). I would work closely with the employee to understand the specific details of their situation and the length of leave they require.

I would then provide the employee with the necessary paperwork and guidance to initiate the leave request. This may include assisting them in completing FMLA or short-term disability forms, if applicable. I would also discuss any available paid time off or other benefits the employee may be able to utilize during their leave.

Throughout the process, I would maintain open communication with the employee to address any concerns or questions they may have. I would also work with their manager to ensure a smooth transition of their work responsibilities and coverage plan during their absence.

Upon the employee's return, I would meet with them to discuss any necessary accommodations or modifications to their work schedule or duties. My goal would be to support the employee, ensure compliance with company policies and legal requirements, and facilitate a successful reintegration back into the workplace.

121. Q: You receive a report that an employee has been observed taking excessive smoke breaks throughout the day, which is disrupting their productivity and the workflow of their team. How would you address this issue?

A: I would first review the company's policies regarding breaks and time away from the workstation. I would then schedule a private meeting with the employee to discuss the concerns that have been raised.

During the meeting, I would:

- Explain the specific issues that have been observed, such as the frequency and duration of the smoke breaks and the impact on their work and the team.

- Remind the employee of the company's policies and expectations around break times and productivity.
- Provide the employee an opportunity to explain their perspective and any challenges they may be facing.

- Work collaboratively with the employee to identify potential solutions, such as adjusting their break schedule, setting clear expectations, or providing additional support or resources.

If the employee's behavior does not improve after the initial discussion, I would issue a written warning outlining the policy violations and the consequences of continued non-compliance. This could include further disciplinary action, such as suspension or termination, if the issues persist.

Throughout the process, I would document all conversations and actions taken, and ensure that the company's policies are being applied consistently. My goal would be to address the performance concerns, support the employee in meeting the company's expectations, and maintain a fair and productive work environment for all.

122. Q: An employee approaches you with concerns about a coworker's inappropriate jokes and comments that they find offensive and demeaning. The employee is hesitant to file a formal complaint. How would you handle this situation?

A: I would first listen empathetically to the employee's concerns and assure them that I take the issue of inappropriate workplace behavior very seriously. I would explain that the company has a zero-tolerance policy for harassment and discrimination, and that all employees have the right to work in a respectful and professional environment.

I would then encourage the employee to provide specific details about the inappropriate comments or jokes, including dates, times, and any witnesses. I would explain that while the employee may not want to file a formal complaint, I still have a responsibility to investigate the matter to ensure the work environment remains safe and inclusive for all. Next, I would schedule a private meeting with the accused coworker to discuss the allegations. I would approach the conversation in a calm and non-confrontational manner, explaining that concerns have been raised about their behavior and that it is unacceptable. I would provide clear examples of the inappropriate comments or jokes, and explain why they are considered offensive and demeaning.

I would then reiterate the company's policies and expectations around professional conduct, and warn the coworker that any further incidents could result in disciplinary action, up to and including termination. I would also encourage the coworker to be more mindful of their words and actions, and to treat all colleagues with respect.

Throughout the process, I would document all discussions and actions taken, and continue to monitor the situation closely. I would also follow up with the initial employee to ensure they feel comfortable in the work environment and that the inappropriate behavior has ceased.

If the issues persist or escalate, I would not hesitate to initiate a formal investigation and take appropriate disciplinary measures against the offending employee, prioritizing the safety and well-being of all employees.

123. Q: You discover that an employee has been accessing and sharing confidential company information without authorization. How would you address this breach of trust?

A: As the HR Manager, I would take this breach of confidentiality very seriously, as it poses significant risks to the company's operations and reputation. I would first review the company's policies and procedures regarding the handling of confidential information, as well as any relevant legal and regulatory requirements.

I would then schedule a private meeting with the employee to discuss the issue. During the meeting, I would:

- Clearly explain the specific instances of unauthorized access and sharing of confidential information that have been identified.

- Remind the employee of the company's policies and their obligations to protect sensitive data.

- Provide the employee an opportunity to explain their actions and understand their perspective.

- Emphasize the gravity of the situation and the potential consequences, such as disciplinary action or even legal liability.

- Inform the employee that the incident will be thoroughly investigated, and that any further violations will result in more severe consequences.

Depending on the severity and nature of the breach, I may also involve other relevant stakeholders, such as the IT department, legal counsel, or senior management, to ensure a comprehensive and appropriate response.

If the investigation confirms the employee's misconduct, I would follow the company's disciplinary procedures, which could range from a formal written warning to termination of employment, depending on the specific circumstances. I would also work with the IT and security teams to implement additional safeguards and monitoring to prevent similar incidents in the future.

Throughout the process, I would maintain strict confidentiality, document all actions taken, and ensure that the employee is treated fairly and with respect, while also upholding the company's policies and protecting its interests.

124. Q: An employee approaches you with concerns about their manager's leadership style, stating that the manager is often unavailable, provides little feedback or direction, and does not effectively manage the team's workload. How would you address this situation?

A: I would first meet privately with the employee to fully understand the specific issues they are experiencing with their manager's leadership style. I would encourage them to provide concrete examples and details about the manager's behaviors and the impact on their work and the team.

Next, I would schedule a meeting with the manager to discuss the employee's concerns. I would approach the conversation in a constructive manner, avoiding accusations and instead focusing on the need to improve the manager-employee relationship and the overall team dynamics.

During the meeting with the manager, I would:

- Share the feedback and concerns raised by the employee, without disclosing their identity.

- Provide the manager an opportunity to share their perspective and understand any challenges they may be facing.

- Collaborate with the manager to identify areas for improvement, such as providing more frequent check-ins, setting clearer expectations and deadlines, or delegating work more effectively.
- Suggest resources, training, or coaching that could help the manager develop their leadership and people management skills.

- Establish a plan of action with specific goals and a timeline for improvement.

I would then follow up with both the employee and the manager to monitor the progress and ensure the situation is improving. If the manager's behavior does not change despite the interventions, I would consider more formal disciplinary actions, up to and including a change in the manager's role or termination, if necessary.

Throughout the process, I would maintain confidentiality, document all discussions and actions taken, and strive to find a resolution that addresses the employee's concerns, supports the manager's development, and fosters a positive and productive work environment.

125. Q: You receive an anonymous complaint alleging that a manager is engaging in favoritism and unfair treatment of certain employees. How would you investigate and address this issue?

A: As an HR Manager, I would take this anonymous complaint very seriously, as allegations of favoritism and unfair treatment can significantly undermine morale, trust, and the overall work environment. I would first review the company's policies and procedures related to performance management, promotions, and disciplinary actions to understand the guidelines and expectations around fair and equitable treatment of employees.

Next, I would launch a thorough and impartial investigation, while maintaining the confidentiality of the complainant. This would involve:

- Reviewing the performance records, disciplinary actions, and promotion histories of the employees under the accused manager's supervision to identify any patterns or discrepancies.

- Conducting confidential interviews with a sample of the manager's direct reports, as well as the manager themselves, to gather more information about the alleged favoritism and unfair treatment.

- Analyzing any available documentation, such as meeting notes, emails, or performance reviews, that could provide further insight into the

126. Q: How do you ensure the HR department is aligned with the company's strategic goals?

A: I regularly communicate with top management to understand the company's strategic goals and align HR initiatives accordingly. This involves developing HR strategies that support business objectives, such as talent acquisition, training programs, and employee engagement initiatives.

127. Q: How do you handle a high turnover rate in a department?

A: I analyze exit interview data to identify common reasons for turnover, address any underlying issues such as management practices or workplace conditions, and develop retention strategies like career development opportunities and employee recognition programs.

128. Q: What strategies do you use to improve employee engagement?

A: I implement regular employee surveys to gather feedback, promote open communication, provide opportunities for professional growth, and recognize and reward employees' achievements to foster a positive work environment.

129. Q: How do you stay updated on labor laws and HR best practices?

A: I subscribe to HR publications, attend relevant workshops and conferences, participate in professional HR associations, and engage in continuous learning through online courses and certifications.

130. Q: How would you address a situation where an employee feels discriminated against?

A: I would ensure a thorough investigation by gathering all facts from the employee, witnesses, and relevant documentation. I would follow the company's anti-discrimination policy, take appropriate action based on findings, and ensure the employee is supported throughout the process.

131. Q: Describe your approach to managing a diverse workforce.

A: I promote an inclusive culture by implementing diversity training, encouraging open dialogue, and creating policies that support diversity and inclusion. I also ensure fair hiring practices and provide equal opportunities for all employees.

132. Q: How do you develop effective training programs?

A: I assess the training needs through employee surveys and performance data, design programs that address skill gaps, use various training methods (e.g., workshops, e-learning), and evaluate the effectiveness through feedback and performance improvements.

133. Q: How do you handle employee grievances?

A: I listen to the employee's concerns with empathy, conduct a thorough investigation, and resolve the issue promptly and fairly, ensuring adherence to company policies and maintaining confidentiality.

134. Q: What steps do you take to ensure compliance with employment regulations?

A: I regularly review and update HR policies to comply with current laws, conduct audits, provide training to managers on legal requirements, and maintain accurate employee records.

135. Q: How do you manage the recruitment process?

A: I create detailed job descriptions, use various sourcing methods to attract candidates, conduct thorough interviews, and collaborate with hiring managers to select the best fit for the company.

136. Q: How do you handle a situation where an employee is underperforming?

A: I identify the root causes of the underperformance, provide feedback and support, develop a performance improvement plan, and monitor progress, offering additional resources as needed.

137. Q: Describe a time when you successfully implemented a new HR initiative.

A: I implemented an employee wellness program that included fitness challenges, mental health resources, and nutritional guidance. This initiative led to increased employee participation and overall improvement in workplace morale.

138. Q: How do you approach succession planning?

A: I identify key roles and potential successors, assess their skills and development needs, and create individual development plans to prepare them for future leadership positions.

139. Q: How do you ensure effective communication within the HR department?

A: I hold regular team meetings, use collaborative tools for information sharing, and maintain open lines of communication to ensure everyone is informed and aligned with department goals.

140. Q: How do you handle confidential information?

A: I strictly adhere to company policies regarding confidentiality, ensure secure storage of sensitive data, and limit access to authorized personnel only.

141. Q: Describe your experience with HR software and tools.

A: I have experience using various HR software such as Workday, SAP SuccessFactors, and BambooHR to manage employee data, streamline processes, and generate reports.

142. Q: How do you handle a situation where a manager is not following HR policies?

A: I address the issue directly with the manager, provide training on the importance of following HR policies, and monitor compliance, taking disciplinary action if necessary.

143. Q: How do you support employee career development?

A: I offer training programs, mentorship opportunities, and career pathing tools to help employees achieve their career goals within the organization.

144. Q: What is your approach to managing employee benefits?

A: I regularly review and benchmark benefits packages to ensure competitiveness, communicate benefits clearly to employees, and assist them in understanding and utilizing their benefits effectively.

145. Q: How do you handle a situation where an employee's behavior is affecting team morale?

A: I address the behavior privately with the employee, provide constructive feedback, and work with them to develop a plan for improvement, monitoring progress and making adjustments as needed.

146. Q: How do you manage organizational change?

A: I communicate changes clearly and transparently, involve employees in the process, provide necessary training, and offer support to help them adapt to new systems and processes.

147. Q: Describe your approach to employee recognition.

A: I implement formal recognition programs, such as Employee of the Month, as well as informal recognition like thank-you notes and public praise, to acknowledge and reward employees' contributions.

148. Q: How do you handle a situation where an employee's personal issues are affecting their work performance?

A: I offer support through employee assistance programs, provide flexible work arrangements if possible, and work with the employee to find solutions that help them balance personal and professional responsibilities.

149. Q: What strategies do you use for conflict resolution?

A: I use active listening, mediation, and negotiation techniques to understand both sides of the conflict, facilitate open communication, and find mutually acceptable solutions.

150. Q: How do you handle the onboarding process for new employees?

A: I ensure new employees have a smooth transition by providing a comprehensive orientation, assigning a mentor, and regularly checking in to address any questions or concerns.

151. Q: How do you manage employee attendance and punctuality issues?

A: I track attendance records, address issues promptly with the employees involved, and implement corrective actions such as counseling or disciplinary measures if necessary.

152. Q: How do you ensure fair and unbiased hiring practices?

A: I implement structured interviews, use diverse hiring panels, and provide training on unconscious bias to ensure a fair and equitable hiring process.

153. Q: How do you handle a situation where an employee's skills no longer meet the company's needs?

A: I assess the employee's skills, provide retraining or upskilling opportunities, and, if necessary, work with them to find a role within the company that better matches their abilities.

154. Q: How do you address employee burnout?

A: I promote a healthy work-life balance, encourage regular breaks, provide mental health resources, and work with managers to ensure workloads are manageable.

155. Q: How do you handle a situation where an employee's compensation is below market rate?

A: I conduct a compensation analysis, present the findings to management, and advocate for adjustments to ensure the employee's pay is competitive and fair.

156. Q: Describe your experience with developing HR policies.

A: I have developed and implemented various HR policies, including employee conduct, remote work, and performance management policies, ensuring they align with legal requirements and company values.

157. Q: How do you handle a situation where an employee's performance review is disputed?

A: I review the performance data, gather additional feedback if necessary, and facilitate a meeting between the employee and their manager to address concerns and find a resolution.

158. Q: How do you promote a positive workplace culture?

A: I encourage open communication, recognize and celebrate achievements, provide opportunities for professional growth, and foster an inclusive and supportive environment.

159. Q: How do you handle a situation where an employee is resistant to change?

A: I understand the reasons behind their resistance, provide clear communication about the benefits of the change, offer support and training, and involve them in the change process to gain their buy-in.

160. Q: How do you ensure continuous improvement in HR processes?

A: I regularly review and evaluate HR processes, gather feedback from employees and managers, and implement changes to improve efficiency and effectiveness.

161. Q: How do you handle a situation where an employee violates the company's code of conduct?

A: I conduct a thorough investigation, gather all relevant information, and take appropriate disciplinary action based on the company's policies, ensuring fairness and consistency.

162. Q: How do you manage employee leave and absence requests?

A: I ensure all requests are documented, review them in line with company policies, and work with managers to ensure business needs are met while accommodating employee needs.

163. Q: How do you handle a situation where an employee is experiencing workplace harassment?

A: I conduct a confidential investigation, take immediate action to stop the harassment, provide support to the affected employee, and ensure compliance with company policies and legal requirements.

164. Q: Describe your approach to talent management.

A: I focus on identifying high-potential employees, providing them with development opportunities, and creating succession plans to ensure a pipeline of future leaders.

165. Q: Describe a time when you had to handle a conflict between two employees. How did you resolve it?

A: I encountered a conflict between two employees over workload distribution. I first met with each employee individually to understand their perspectives. Then, I facilitated a joint meeting where both parties could express their concerns openly. We collaborated to redistribute tasks more equitably and set clear expectations for future communication. Follow-up meetings ensured the resolution was effective.

166. Q: Can you give an example of how you've helped improve employee retention in a previous role?

A: In my previous role, I implemented an employee recognition program that celebrated both small and large achievements. This initiative, along with regular career development workshops, significantly boosted employee morale and reduced turnover by 15% within a year.

167. Q: How do you handle confidential information when dealing with sensitive employee issues?

A: Handling confidential information requires strict adherence to privacy policies. I ensure that all sensitive discussions are conducted in private, secure locations, and I limit access to information only to those who absolutely need to know. Documentation is stored securely, and electronic data is encrypted to prevent unauthorized access.

168. Q: Describe a time when you had to implement a new HR policy that was met with resistance. How did you manage the situation?

A: When rolling out a new remote work policy, there was significant resistance due to concerns about productivity. I organized information sessions to explain the benefits, addressed concerns transparently, and gathered feedback for adjustments. By involving employees in the process and demonstrating leadership support, acceptance gradually increased.

169. Q: Have you ever had to mediate a dispute involving a manager and their direct report? How did you handle it?

A: Yes, I mediated a dispute where a manager and their direct report disagreed on performance expectations. I conducted separate interviews to understand both sides and then facilitated a meeting where each party could communicate their viewpoints. We established a clear performance plan and set regular check-ins to ensure ongoing alignment and improvement.

170. Q: Can you provide an example of a time when you had to adapt quickly to a significant change in your organization?

A: During a major organizational restructure, I had to quickly adapt by reassessing workforce needs and reallocating resources. I coordinated with department heads to identify critical roles and provided support to employees transitioning to new positions. Clear communication and proactive support were key to ensuring a smooth transition.

171. Q: How do you stay current with changes in employment law and HR best practices?

A: I stay current by subscribing to professional HR journals, participating in webinars, attending industry conferences, and being an active member of professional HR organizations like SHRM. Regular training and continuous education ensure that I am up-to-date with the latest trends and legal requirements.

172. Q: Describe a time when you successfully led a team through a challenging project.

A: I led a team through the implementation of a new HRIS system, which was a significant change from our previous processes. By breaking down the project into manageable phases, providing comprehensive training, and maintaining open lines of communication, we successfully completed the project on time and within budget, improving overall efficiency.

173. Q: How do you approach diversity and inclusion in the workplace?

A: I believe in creating a diverse and inclusive workplace by promoting unbiased recruitment practices, implementing diversity training programs, and establishing employee resource groups. Regularly reviewing our policies and practices helps ensure they support a culture of inclusion and respect for all employees.

174. Q: Tell me about a time you had to manage an underperforming employee. What steps did you take?

A: I managed an underperforming employee by first conducting a performance review to identify specific areas of concern. We then developed a performance improvement plan with clear, achievable goals and regular check-ins. Providing additional training and resources, along with ongoing feedback, helped the employee improve their performance over time.

175. Q: Can you describe an experience where you improved an HR process? What was the result?

A: I identified inefficiencies in our onboarding process, which led to delays in new hires becoming productive. I streamlined the process by introducing an online onboarding portal, which included all necessary forms, training modules, and a virtual tour. This improvement reduced onboarding time by 40% and enhanced the new hire experience.

176. Q: How do you handle a situation where an employee complains about discrimination or harassment?

A: I take complaints about discrimination or harassment very seriously. I would conduct a thorough and impartial investigation, ensuring confidentiality and protection for the complainant. Based on the findings, appropriate actions would be taken, including disciplinary measures if necessary, and measures would be put in place to prevent future incidents.

177. Q: Give an example of how you have managed a reduction in workforce.

A: During a company downsizing, I managed the workforce reduction by developing a fair and transparent process. I communicated openly with employees about the reasons behind the decision, provided support through career counseling and outplacement services, and ensured that the affected employees were treated with dignity and respect.

178. Q: How do you ensure that your HR practices align with the strategic goals of the organization?

A: I ensure alignment by actively collaborating with senior leadership to understand the organization's strategic goals. I then translate these goals into HR initiatives and policies that support business objectives, such as talent acquisition strategies that match the company's growth plans and development programs that enhance key competencies.

179. Q: Describe a time when you had to address a significant change in employment law that affected your organization.

A: When a significant change in employment law regarding overtime pay was introduced, I quickly updated our payroll systems and policies to ensure compliance. I held training sessions for managers and employees to explain the changes and their implications, and worked closely with our legal team to audit our practices and mitigate any risks.

180. Q: How do you handle the challenge of recruiting in a highly competitive market?

A: In a highly competitive market, I focus on creating a strong employer brand that highlights our unique value proposition. I leverage social media, employee referrals, and partnerships with universities to attract top talent. Offering competitive compensation packages and a positive candidate experience also helps us stand out from competitors.

181. Q: Can you provide an example of a successful employee engagement initiative you have led?

A: I led a successful employee engagement initiative by introducing a flexible working hours policy, which was highly appreciated by the staff. Additionally, we launched a monthly town hall meeting where employees could voice their opinions and suggestions. These initiatives resulted in a noticeable increase in employee satisfaction and a 10% improvement in our engagement survey scores.

182. Q: How do you approach performance reviews to ensure they are effective and fair?

A: I ensure performance reviews are effective and fair by implementing a structured, competency-based assessment process. Managers are trained to provide constructive feedback and set clear, achievable goals. Regular check-ins throughout the year, rather than annual reviews alone, help in continuous performance improvement and development.

183. Q: Describe a time when you had to manage an HR crisis. How did you handle it?

A: During a data breach incident, I had to manage the HR crisis by promptly informing all employees and coordinating with IT to secure the data. I provided guidance on protecting personal information, offered credit monitoring services, and implemented stricter data protection measures. Transparency and swift action were key to maintaining trust and minimizing impact.

184. Q: How do you handle a situation where an employee is consistently late to work?

A: I would address the issue by meeting with the employee to understand the reasons behind their tardiness. Together, we would develop a plan to improve punctuality, which might include adjusting work hours or providing resources like transportation assistance. Consistent follow-up would ensure the issue is resolved.

185. Q: Can you give an example of how you've promoted work-life balance in your organization?

A: I promoted work-life balance by introducing flexible working arrangements, such as telecommuting and flexible hours. We also offered wellness programs, including stress management workshops and fitness classes. These initiatives helped reduce burnout and increased overall employee satisfaction and productivity.

186. Q: How do you manage the onboarding process to ensure new hires integrate smoothly?

A: I manage the onboarding process by providing a comprehensive orientation program that includes an overview of company culture, values, and expectations. New hires are paired with mentors to guide them through their initial days. Regular check-ins during the first few months ensure they feel supported and integrated into the team.

187. Q: Describe a situation where you had to manage a cross-functional team for an HR project.

A: I managed a cross-functional team to develop a new performance management system. By fostering open communication, clearly defining roles, and leveraging each team member's expertise, we successfully delivered the project on time. The new system improved performance tracking and employee development across the organization.

188. Q: How do you handle feedback from employees about HR policies that they find unfair or problematic?

A: I handle feedback by actively listening to employees' concerns and thoroughly reviewing the policies in question. I ensure that their feedback is considered in any revisions, and I communicate any changes transparently. This approach not only addresses the concerns but also shows that the organization values employee input.

189. Q: Can you describe an experience where you improved communication within your HR team?

A: I improved communication within my HR team by implementing weekly team meetings and using collaborative tools like Slack for real-time updates. I encouraged an open-door policy and fostered a culture of transparency, where team members felt comfortable sharing ideas and concerns. Additionally, I introduced a shared project management tool to track tasks and deadlines, which helped everyone stay informed and aligned. This approach not only streamlined our workflows but also enhanced team cohesion and morale.

190. Q: Describe a time when you had to coach a manager on how to handle a difficult employee situation.

A: A manager was struggling with an employee who consistently missed deadlines. I coached the manager on effective communication techniques, including how to provide constructive feedback and set clear expectations. We role-played the conversation, and I provided tools for ongoing performance monitoring. The manager successfully addressed the issue, and the employee's performance improved as a result.

191. Q: How do you ensure that training programs are effective and meet the needs of the organization?

A: I ensure training programs are effective by conducting thorough needs assessments to identify skill gaps and aligning training objectives with organizational goals. I use a mix of training methods, including workshops, e-learning, and on-the-job training, and regularly collect feedback to make necessary adjustments. Post-training evaluations help measure the impact on performance and productivity.

192. Q: Can you provide an example of how you've handled a situation where an employee's values did not align with the company's culture?

A: An employee's behavior was consistently at odds with our collaborative culture. I had a candid conversation with the employee to understand their perspective and shared examples of expected behaviors. We discussed how their actions were impacting the team and explored ways they could align better with our values. Despite efforts to support the employee, they ultimately decided to leave the organization, recognizing it was not the right fit for them.

193. Q: Describe a time when you implemented a change that improved the overall efficiency of the HR department.

A: I implemented an electronic document management system to replace our paper-based processes. This change significantly reduced the time spent on administrative tasks, improved data accuracy, and enhanced document accessibility. As a result, the HR team could focus more on strategic initiatives, increasing overall efficiency by 30%.

194. Q: How do you handle situations where you need to enforce unpopular policies?

A: Enforcing unpopular policies requires clear communication and empathy. I explain the reasons behind the policy, how it aligns with organizational goals, and the benefits it brings in the long term. I also listen to employee concerns and offer support to help them adapt to the changes. Transparency and support are crucial to gaining acceptance and compliance.

195. Question: Can you provide an example of how you've used data and analytics to improve HR processes?

A: I used data analytics to identify patterns in employee turnover, revealing that a significant number of exits occurred within the first six months. Based on this insight, I revamped the onboarding program to include more comprehensive training and mentoring. This data-driven approach reduced early turnover by 20%, saving costs and improving retention.

196. Q: How do you manage the performance and development of your HR team?

A: I manage my team's performance and development through regular one-on-one meetings, where we discuss progress, challenges, and career aspirations. I provide ongoing feedback and opportunities for professional growth, such as training and certifications. Setting clear goals and recognizing achievements ensures that team members stay motivated and continuously improve.

197. Q: Describe a time when you had to handle an unexpected HR crisis.

A: During a sudden company merger, employees were anxious about job security and organizational changes. I managed the crisis by providing timely and transparent communication, organizing Q&A sessions with leadership, and setting up a support system for affected employees. This proactive approach helped maintain trust and morale during a turbulent period.

198. Q: How do you foster a culture of continuous learning in your organization?

A: I foster a culture of continuous learning by promoting and supporting professional development opportunities, such as workshops, online courses, and conferences. I encourage knowledge sharing through regular lunch-and-learn sessions and cross-departmental projects. Additionally, I recognize and reward employees who actively seek to enhance their skills and contribute to their colleagues' learning.

199. Q: Can you give an example of how you've managed HR compliance in a rapidly changing regulatory environment?

A: In a rapidly changing regulatory environment, I ensured HR compliance by staying informed through continuous education and legal updates. I collaborated with our legal team to review and update our policies regularly. Additionally, I conducted training sessions for managers and employees to ensure everyone understood and adhered to the new regulations, minimizing compliance risks.

200. Q: Describe a situation where you had to support an employee through a personal crisis.

A: An employee was going through a difficult divorce, which affected their performance. I offered support by connecting them with our Employee Assistance Program (EAP) and providing flexible working arrangements. I maintained open communication to check on their well-being and ensured they felt supported during this challenging time.